WESTMAR COLLE

O9-BHK-480

THE CHAUTAUQUA MOVEMENT

WESTMAR COLLEGE LIBRARY

THE CHAUTAUQUA MOVEMENT

An Episode in the Continuing American Revolution

JOSEPH E. GOULD

STATE UNIVERSITY OF NEW YORK PRESS
ALBANY

374.29
G697

LC
6551
.G6

PUBLISHED BY STATE UNIVERSITY OF NEW YORK PRESS
THURLOW TERRACE, ALBANY, NEW YORK 12201

COPYRIGHT © 1961 BY THE STATE UNIVERSITY OF NEW YORK
ALL RIGHTS RESERVED

SECOND PAPERBOUND PRINTING, 1970

LIBRARY OF CONGRESS CATALOG CARD NUMBER 61-8734
STANDARD BOOK NUMBER 87395-004-6
MANUFACTURED IN THE UNITED STATES OF AMERICA

83438

For Phyllis

Foreword

In *The Chautauqua Movement* I have tried to set forth the beginnings of the most significant venture in popular education in the United States, and to place it in its proper setting in the history of our country.

Through the activities of the Chautauqua Institution, the great world was opened up to the incredibly isolated communities of our then new Middle West. Inaugurated for the purpose of training Sunday school teachers, the Institution rapidly expanded its course offerings and its popular appeal until it reached into thousands of culture-starved communities and helped give discipline and direction to angry and inchoate movements of social protest. Its influence on the founding and early years of one of our greatest universities significantly shaped the present pattern of American higher education.

The Chautauqua movement was not a single, unified, coherent plan, developed and directed by one man or a group of men. It was, fundamentally, a response to an unspoken demand, a sensitive alertness to the cravings of millions of people for "something better." It was a part of that tradition of revolution without dogma that has been typical of America since the first settlers landed on our shores. One of several waves of mass enthusiasm for self-improvement, social betterment, and reform that have periodically swept over our nation, the Chautauqua movement left behind changed tastes, changed laws, and changed social habits.

Specifically, the Chautauqua movement pioneered in correspondence courses, lecture-study groups, and reading circles in the United States. It filled a vast need for adult education opportunities, predominantly in the rural regions of America. Chautauqua and its imitators also provided a free platform for the discussion of vital issues at a critical time in our history, and a high standard for cultural entertainment in an era when men hungered for good music, "book learning," and lectures in a way which we cannot imagine today.

The Chautauqua movement introduced many other new educational concepts, ideas, and opportunities to American life: university extension courses; summer sessions; civic music and civic opera associations; Boy Scouts, Camp Fire Girls, and similar youth groups; courses in dietetics, nutrition, library science, physical education; a university press. Dozens of such ideas, germinated in the minds of liberal-thinking Americans, were given their most vigorous and effective support from Chautauqua platforms. Brilliant, well-informed men and women lectured to avidly listening crowds on such topics as the conservation of natural resources, the eight-hour day, woman suffrage, pure food and drug legislation, national forests and parks, slum clearance, city planning, direct election of United States senators, the regulation of interstate commerce, and the cooperative movement.

When the vigor of the Chautauqua movement declined

after the First World War, an important episode in the continuing American revolution had been completed and the cultural gap between a rural Midwestern population and that of the more advantageously situated East had been narrowed significantly. Chautauqua played a major role in this phenomenal awakening—termed by Frederick Lewis Allen "The Great Change."

J. E. G.

Contents

Illustrations

xiii

Photograph of Rockefeller and Harper reprinted by courtesy of the Rockefeller Foundation; all other photographs are from the collection at the Chautauqua Institution Library, reproduced by courtesy of the Chautauqua Institution, Chautauqua, New York

The
Chautauqua Movement

I Birth of a Movement

In the rolling hills of southwestern New York State, just before they descend sharply to Lake Erie, there is a lake named Chautauqua. An odd name, certainly, not really pleasant to the ear, yet millions of people once knew of it and talked about it. For a period of time in our history, Chautauqua was one of the most famous places in the nation.

It was in the summer of 1874 that two middle-aged gentlemen of the Methodist persuasion started what we would now call a "camp" at Fair Point on Chautauqua Lake and, quite without meaning to, created the most vigorous private movement in popular education the world has ever seen.

The history of Chautauqua's founding is simply told. The basic idea was in no way a radical departure from custom. John Heyl Vincent, a clergyman who had never attended college as a resident student, had become secretary of the Methodist Sunday School Union in 1868. Vincent, later a bishop in his church, had been a circuit rider at the age of nineteen. He had served pastorates in Illinois since 1857. In 1868 he established the *Sunday School Quarterly*, a journal devoted to the promotion of higher standards in Sunday school teaching; in 1869 the Methodist high command chose him as the first General Agent of that church's Sunday School Union.

Vincent was concerned with the problem of securing good Sunday school instruction from untrained and sometimes unlearned lay men and women, and he promoted the formation of Sunday School Institutes—intensive short-term courses for religious teachers comparable to the Normal Institutes which many communities were holding for public school teachers at that time. These were two-day affairs. Vincent had hopes for an institute less limited in time and with greater instructional resources.

Sometime before 1868 Dr. Vincent met Lewis Miller, a prosperous Akron manufacturer, whose avocation was Sunday school work. Miller had designed and built a Sunday school hall for the First Methodist Church in Akron which was widely copied, and the two men recognized that they shared many ideas concerning the value of Sunday school instruction and the necessity for securing good teachers. Vincent proposed his scheme for a protracted normal institute for Sunday school workers and suggested it be held in the new building in Akron. Miller had a better idea. Why not set up the institute in some natural beauty spot, perhaps on the shores of a lake? A camp-meeting site on the shore of Chautauqua Lake in western New York was investigated by the two men and found to be eminently satisfactory. Vincent was disturbed by the possibility that the location might make many associate the new Chautauqua venture with camp-meeting revivalism, but Miller insisted that there would be no such association because the kind of assembly he proposed would rigorously exclude camp-meeting features.

The first Assembly opened at Fair Point on Chautauqua Lake on August 4, 1874, and continued for two weeks. The program for each week was divided into six sections and included practical exhibits and specimen Sunday school meetings. One of the practical exhibits was a huge contour map of Palestine, laid out on the lake shore. This map is still in use.

In addition to instructional classes, Dr. Vincent had planned an elaborate recreational program. Students whose energies flagged after intensive sessions devoted to the problems of Sunday school organization and management were refreshed in dozens of ways. Lighthearted games were skillfully mixed in with inspirational lectures by the famous platform personality John B. Gough. Dr. E. O. Haven, of newly founded Syracuse University, lent an academic flavor to the proceedings, and the evenings were made enjoyable by concerts, illuminations, and displays of fireworks.

The 1874 Assembly, first of a series that has continued in unbroken succession to the present day, was an unqualified success. Those who attended were enthusiastic, and with good reason. They had come in contact with a truly great personality—Dr. John Heyl Vincent—good reason for them to want to come back and to persuade others to come too.[1]

John Vincent was a most unusual man. He had been born in 1832 in Tuscaloosa, Alabama, of Northern parents, and he grew to manhood in Pennsylvania. His parents, one Presbyterian, one Lutheran, became Methodists in Alabama; his grandfather had been a friend and admirer of the Unitarian scientist Joseph Priestley. Perhaps these circumstances explain why Vincent was singularly free from the narrow sectional prejudice and the religious dogmatism verging on bigotry which were all too common in his day. He had a deep reverence and love for learning, and although he had been unable to attend college, few college graduates were more widely read than he. He had had the opportunity for extensive travel abroad and his notes show him to be a keen and careful observer.[2]

Tolerant and reserved in his judgments, he still had strong convictions. He had been eleven years old when the Millerites terrified the immature and unstable by their lugubrious preparations for the Day of Judgment. The child had been frightened by this nonsense and the grown man vigorously rejected the concept of God as a petulant and vengeful deity. Vincent believed that "religion, rightly understood, should be essentially cheerful and optimistic." [3] His great aim in life, for himself and for all who would learn from him, was right understanding of Christianity and of everything pertaining to it.

Dr. Vincent was a modest man and he had no desire to build at Chautauqua a stage set in which he could play the lion. Instead, he looked about for someone who could excite and inspire his 1875 Assembly, someone whose name would be on everyone's lips. His choice was Henry Ward Beecher. Beecher, it developed, was not available. A sensational lawsuit had been brought against him that year by a man named Theodore Tilton and he therefore could not come to Chautauqua.

Dr. Vincent was still determined to secure a celebrity for his 1875 Assembly, and he finally decided upon an old friend of his Illinois days, now famous as Ulysses Simpson Grant, eighteenth President of the United States. Vincent sent the Reverend T. H. Flood, pastor of the First Methodist Church of Jamestown, off to Long Branch, New Jersey, where the President was resting, to invite him to Chautauqua. Grant accepted readily, and it was planned that he should arrive in Jamestown Saturday noon, August 14, and stay the weekend at Chautauqua.

On the date appointed, Grant arrived by rail from Long Branch, and after luncheon with former Governor Fenton, he was escorted up the lake by a flotilla of eleven gaily trimmed steamboats. The President's craft, the *Josie Belle*, had been elaborately decorated by the Clotho Society of Dr. Flood's church. Grant sat in an armchair in the bow of the *Josie Belle* and listened to the Mayville Band as his boat steamed along majestically. Throngs lined the Narrows and the crowd of fifteen thousand that greeted the President when he disembarked at Chautauqua "seemed to form itself into one mammoth handkerchief and one throat that sent up shout after shout." [4]

Grant's visit gave Chautauqua excellent nationwide publicity. In recalling the event seventeen years later, when Chautauqua had in truth become a household word, Dr. Flood wrote:

> An agent of the Associated Press and a number of staff correspondents from great daily papers in the chief cities were in the President's party. In their published dispatches and letters, these men gave picturesque accounts of Chautauqua, what it was, its personnel, the program, the place, and its attractions. [5]

Eighteen hundred seventy-six and 1877 were years of steady growth at Chautauqua: enrollment more than doubled each year. First Hebrew, then Greek, were added to the curriculum. Then, on August 10, 1878, Dr. Vincent rather diffidently announced to the nearly five hundred persons who attended the fifth Chautauqua Assembly his plan for the formation of a study group that would embark on a four-year program of guided reading. This group, to be called the Chautauqua Literary and Scientific Circle, would, he hoped, number at least ten.

Two hundred signed up during the first hour. More than 8,400 persons, most of them from the new states of the Midwest, joined Circles in 1878. Within ten years the enrollment climbed to 100,000, and at least that many more had either dropped out or completed their four-year course.

The reading list for the first year of the course was ambitious, but it made sense to the thousands who saw it described in the pages of the *Sunday School Journal* and "sent in" for the books and manuals. It included Green's *Short History of the English People*, Mahaffey's *Old Greek Life*, Brooke's *Primer of English Literature*, two books on the Bible, one on astronomy, and one on physiology, plus study guides for each.

The eagerness with which people in the new, raw Midwest seized upon this opportunity for self-education has been sketched compassionately by Zona Gale:

> I remember sitting silent on a little carpet-covered stool and listening to a woman relate to my mother a part of the epilogue to the American Revolution:
> "And, look here, in the first place they never wanted to unite at

all! No, Sir! Some of 'em said it was impossible the colonies should ever be got to unite. Yes, Sir! And when they first talked it, to a meeting in Albany, only seven colonies sent delegates and nobody much but Benjamin Franklin was what you might say hot for it. Did you ever hear of such a thing? But the Governor of Massachusetts, he wanted it in order to fight France. And say! the folks in Massachusetts was jealous of the folks in Virginia, and Georgia and South Carolina most fit over using the Savannah River. And Mrs. Gale, when them British troops came over they tented 'em in Boston Common, and our book says Samuel Adams got up in the Old South Church and he says 'this meeting can do nothing more to save the country.' . . . wait 'til I tell you: that was when we dumped the tea—wasn't it grand? "

. . . all her facts had been unknown earth until the Chautauqua American History had opened to her. And now gossip, domestic grievances, prices, had all been dropped from her conversation . . . all the stimuli were there—the love of learning, latent in the pioneer and waiting the mellower time when it might flower; the social urge to work together; the zest of competition in the race for seals and courses completed, and tenderest of all, the dumb desire to "keep up" with the young folk, already coming home from school with challenging inquiries.[6]

In an incredibly short period of time, nearly every community of any size in the United States had at least one person following the Chautauqua reading program as a member of C.L.S.C. Iowa had more than one hundred Circles in 1885, more than half of these in the city of Des Moines. Travelers reported finding train crews on western railroads who had constituted themselves a Circle, and there were crossroads storekeepers who dragooned their cracker-barrel philosophers into joining C.L.S.C., giving form and purpose to the traditional desultory conversations. The *Chautauquan*, a monthly magazine, was established for C.L.S.C.

members in 1880; within a short time it had a circulation rivaling the most popular magazines of the day.

It was natural that interested persons who lived at some distance from the original Chautauqua Assembly should consider banding together to create something like it in a more accessible spot. Assemblies (sometimes called "little Chautauquas") began to spring up all over the Midwest. They varied widely in size, in program, and in denominational or other sponsorship, but they had certain basic features in common. Automatically, it would seem, the reputation for quality, respectability, and integrity that the original Chautauqua had earned was inherited with the name. Healthy fun, wholesome recreation, religious reverence, good taste, and honest inquiry—these qualities were associated in the public mind with the word "Chautauqua," and the hundreds of self-styled Chautauquas that were founded by private groups, communities, and religious denominations benefited by this association, although in point of fact none of them was ever in any sense a branch of the original.

By 1890 the number of "independents," as they came to be called, approached two hundred. They were, as often as possible, located near water and a grove of trees. Their programs ranged from a tightly packed five-day assembly to a month or even more of lectures, concerts, courses, and recreation; some of them sponsored a program of correspondence or extension studies in imitation of developments at Chautauqua Lake. The directors of the independents found lecturers, discussion leaders, and teachers among the holidaying faculty members of colleges and universities, and although many of these men and women did not enjoy the reputation and prestige of those whom Dr. Vincent was able to attract to Chautauqua, they all shared an enthusiasm for learning and a distrust of economic and social panaceas.

In retrospect, it is not difficult to discern the appeal that the Chautauqua movement had for the American, particularly the Midwesterner, of the seventies and eighties. The homesteaders in the new states of the Great Plains had been caught up in a movement without pattern. Too frequently, lured by the glowingly optimistic railroad advertisements, the settler and his family had been dropped at some railhead on the vast treeless expanse of the Great Plains and there left to his own devices. The communities he found in existence were lacking in the most rudimentary amenities and a cultural link with the East was out of the question; only the mining communities that had "struck it rich" could afford to underwrite the cost of Eastern "talent." The homesteader's land was held in fief to a bank or a railroad, and the true lords of creation were the Eastern magnates for whose benefit the land and the people were being exploited. Unlike the pre-Civil War pioneer in the old Northwest Territory, who was politically, economically, and socially the equal of his fellow countrymen in any other region, the homesteader felt himself the victim of the banks, the railroads, and the trusts.[7]

The Chautauqua movement offered the discouraged settlers of the new West a link with the heritage they felt they had lost. The books and the lessons widened the narrow circle of their lives, and they sought to find in their courses of study a set of unchanging principles that could guide them through their difficulties.

Thus, at a time when many of the disillusioned settlers of the new Western lands were convinced that they were at best the stepchildren of the Republic, the project that had begun so modestly at Chautauqua in 1874 grew into a grass-roots movement which was to give hope and dignity to the hitherto frustrated ambitions of hundreds of thousands. It guided and stimulated them in their desire to know, and encouraged them to build for themselves free forums for the discussion of subjects of vital interest and for the introduction of new and exciting ideas.

William R. Harper: Young Man in a Hurry

Developments at Chautauqua were rapid following the announcement in 1878 of the Chautauqua Literary and Scientific Circles. In 1879 the Chautauqua Teachers Retreat (later called the School of Pedagogy) was organized, as was the Chautauqua School of Languages. The School of Theology opened in the summer of 1881, and on March 30, 1883, the New York State Legislature recognized "The Chautauqua University" and granted it the right to confer degrees. In less than ten years, what began as a modest project for improving the quality of teaching in Sunday schools was now a full-fledged university, although uniquely different from any other university in the world. This in itself was sufficiently miraculous. Certainly no one would have been hardy enough to predict that this freak among universities would put the stamp of its own uniqueness on all of American higher education. But that is what happened, and here Fate uniquely combined character, chance, and circumstance.

In the early spring of 1883, a committee of Baptists projected the establishment of their own "Chautauqua" on a spot directly across the lake from the Chautauqua Assembly. While Dr. Vincent had generously aided many of the hundreds of "little Chautauquas" (or independents) which had sprung up throughout the Midwest, this one was a little too close for comfort. He could not bring himself to an active discouragement of this worthy effort, but he recognized in it a potential rival. The Baptist denomination was the most numerous in the United States and could, if its efforts were coordinated, throw massive support behind such an enterprise.

We see astuteness linked to cynicism so frequently that we are always surprised when a man of high principles behaves shrewdly. John Heyl Vincent, that most ethical of men, was nevertheless (and why not?) extremely canny. He decided that the most vigorous and promising young educator the Baptists had was a man named William Rainey Harper, so he hired him to teach classes in Hebrew at Chautauqua.

William Rainey Harper, just turned twenty-seven, was born in Muskingum County, Ohio, on July 24, 1856, in the village of New Concord, where his father had operated a drygoods store since 1848.

"Willie," as he was called, was something of a prodigy. He learned to read at a tender age and was ready for the preparatory department of Muskingum College at the age of eight. Muskingum College was a small denominational college in New Concord. Its chief function was preparing local youth for the ministry. As a consequence, its curriculum, both in the preparatory and college departments, was heavily loaded with languages so that prospective ministers might study the Bible in its earliest forms. Mathematics was offered through the calculus, but what science there was was woefully scant. Labeled Natural Philosophy, it apparently consisted of supervised examination of certain "cabinets" containing collections of rock specimens, fossils, and the like.

Dr. David Paul, president of Muskingum College from 1865 to 1879, and related to the Harpers by marriage, took an interest in Willie, finding him equipped with a lightning-fast mind and a prodigious memory. Young Harper took the prescribed course of study and in 1870 was ready for graduation at the age of thirteen. Literally by chance, his future career as an Hebraist was decided when the Class of 1870 cast lots to see who should deliver the Hebrew oration; the choice fell on Harper. His teacher, Dr. F. M. Spencer, later president of Muskingum (1879–86), was not impressed with the perfection of the performance. He wrote: "Every linguist will understand that it would have been impossible for a boy of fourteen [*sic*] to have written and delivered a lengthy oration in Hebrew with the proper use of nouns and verbs."

For the next three years Harper remained in New Concord, clerking in his father's store. This could not have been an irksome task for this gregarious man for the village store was the center of activity, and Harper's later life indicated his fondness for being at the center of an immense bustle. No task was ever irksome to this human dynamo until failing health began to deplete his energies when he was in his late forties.

In the winter of 1872–73, young Harper was given the opportunity to teach a small class in Hebrew at Muskingum

College.[1] He was successful, and Dr. Paul encouraged him to go to Yale for graduate work under William Dwight Whitney. His father fell in with the plan, but with what enthusiasm no one knows. Samuel Harper's diary records, without comment, the fact that Willie's two years at Yale cost him $1,141.73, including railroad fare.

The Yale years opened up a new vista to young Harper. He went there a boy-wonder and found himself only moderately well-prepared for his graduate study. It was characteristic of him, however, that he applied himself with energy to his tasks and soon made up for the inadequacies of his Muskingum preparation. Unfortunately, there is a dearth of material concerning this period of his life. We do know that he worked hard and that he received his degree, a Ph.D. in philology, in June, 1875. He must have been exposed to the growing enthusiasm for the application of philological research to the problems of history and archaeology, but apparently the exposure did not, at that time, awaken a corresponding enthusiasm in him. In 1906 E. Benjamin Andrews, writing his reminiscences of Harper, remembers him as being, in 1876, primarily a grammarian:

> His interests were not speculative, but concrete. So far as I can recall, he relished the classic tongues less because of the history and literature to be got at through them than as a field for the application of his grammatical knowledge in reading by himself and in drilling others.[2]

Upon graduation from Yale, Harper accepted the principalship of a "college" in Macon, Tennessee. This institution, known as Masonic College, boasted seventy-five pupils, none of whom was pursuing college-level work. This experience made a lasting impression on Harper, as witness his fulminations in later life directed at inadequately supported institutions misrepresenting themselves as colleges.

In November, 1875, Harper obtained a leave from his post and married Miss Ella Paul, daughter of President Paul of Muskingum College. The young couple returned to Tennessee and since Harper had no class in Hebrew to teach, he taught his wife. Mrs. Harper, being the daughter of a pedagogue, accepted her fate with good grace and acquired a facility in Hebrew that later must have been unique even among faculty wives.

The following year Harper returned to Ohio. Henry A. Rogers, whom he had known at Yale, was principal of the preparatory department at Denison University, a small Baptist college in Granville, Ohio, and he invited Harper to join his staff as a teacher of Greek and Latin.

When Harper joined the Denison faculty he had just turned twenty and his colleagues were much older men. President Andrews termed the faculty of the preparatory department "teaching talent of the first order, not surpassed by any with which I have ever been acquainted. . . . The gentlemen with whom Harper was thrown in contact and compared upon coming to Granville, while able and willing to help him, were of a character to have discouraged a weaker man."

Harper, however, was quite undismayed. He applied himself to his new task with efficiency and energy and quickly dispelled the misgivings with which some members of the faculty regarded his appointment. He acquitted himself so well that upon Rogers' resignation he was promoted to the principalship of the academic department.

During his tenure at Granville, Harper became a member of the Baptist denomination, being baptized in February, 1877, by immersion. His approach to this change in his religious affiliation was simple and direct. He is reported to have said: "I am not a Christian, but I want to be one, and I mean to be one."

It is tempting to speculate upon the reasons for Harper's conversion and his choice of the Baptist denomination. Soberly, it should be remembered that although he was three years married and the possessor of a doctorate in philology, he was only twenty-two and was serving at a Baptist institution. Hitherto he had not had time to give much attention to organized religion; thus, when he began to feel the need to associate himself with an organized Christian body, it was natural for him to choose that one to which most of his associates belonged. There are other possible reasons, perhaps less pertinent. One is that he may have been attracted by the strong emotional attitude traditional among Baptists, for although his later writing argues in favor of an intellectual approach to religion, he was himself among the most emotional of men, as is shown by his deep attachment to his friends, his love of congenial company, his gregariousness, and the fact that his own personal faith in God, while buttressed by his researches, transcended proof or dogma. Certainly the individualism of the Baptist approach appealed to him. But perhaps most important of all is the fact that President Andrews of Denison was a Baptist. A friendship which was to last for life had grown up between the older and the younger man, and Harper's personal admiration for Andrews was deep and strong. In any case, when Harper was baptized, a chain of events that was to make him president of the University of Chicago began to be forged.

Sixteen months after Harper became a Baptist, he was nominated to fill a vacancy in the department of Hebrew in the Baptist Union Theological Seminary at Morgan Park, Illinois. He was attracted by the position. Hebrew was his first love, and although he was teaching an informal class at Granville, as he had at New Concord, he recognized that only at a theological seminary could he hope to find a full-time position teaching Hebrew. He moved to Morgan Park and took up his duties there on January 1, 1879.

Harper charged into his teaching with the same energy and singleness of purpose that had characterized his efforts at Granville—only now he was teaching his beloved Hebrew. Soon after his arrival, an examining committee of visiting pastors said of his teaching:

> The students at Morgan Park pursue Hebrew as though their immediate settlement in the Pastorate and their final success in the ministry depended upon a knowledge of the entire Hebrew Bible, even to the minutest points.

Eri B. Hulbert, who came to Morgan Park the following year as professor of Church History, seems to have looked upon Harper's zeal with a somewhat jaundiced eye, perhaps because students were skimping their preparation in his field in favor of Hebrew. He writes:

> Such were the singleness and exclusiveness of his aims that neighboring interests were left unnoted. He was little mindful of the bodily welfare of his students; of their undue attention to a single study; of their neglect of other branches; of the consequent lack of balance in their clerical training; of the ill effect of this on their future ministry . . . Many then did not see, and do not even yet

see, that their ministerial preparation would have been more wisely made if their devotion to linguistics had been less excessive. Their instructor, in after years, with vision clarified and judgment matured, went so far as to make Hebrew itself an optional study. Youthful enthusiasm later reflection sobered and regulated.[3]

At the time, however, Harper's energy seemed to know no bounds, and his "youthful enthusiasm" was equally boundless. The minutes of the Board of Trustees of the Baptist Theological Union, the governing board of the seminary, bear this notation for May, 1881: "During Christmas vacation a class of six met the Professor and read the Hebrew Bible at sight eight hours per day for ten days, and a second class read two hours daily."

Incredible as it may seem, Harper proposed the same kind of endurance feat for the summer. He applied to the trustees for, and received, the use of the Seminary building for the summer of 1881. Response from the students was immediate and gratifying. Twenty-three presented themselves, additional teachers had to be secured, and a boarding department was organized. In the summer of 1882 the enrollment increased to sixty-five, and in 1883 eighty-five students registered.

Other summer schools were organized at Worcester, Massachusetts, at New Haven, and at Philadelphia. Harper visited these in his "spare time," organizing teaching staffs and inspiring all concerned with the supreme necessity of learning Hebrew. His most intensive efforts were reserved for Morgan Park, however. Hulbert states in wonder (and we can share his amazement):

Think of a class of beginners in Hebrew reciting four hours a day, and five days in the week, and through a stretch of ten weeks.

Think of the heavy discount on eating, sleeping, exercise, rest and recreation which this prolonged memory tug and this unremitting mental tension necessarily exacted. Think of the magnetic or hypnotic power of a teacher who could entice a crowd of graybeards and youth, of pastors and students, of parents and their children, of matrons and young girls, into such a class.

This was the peripatetic athlete of the classroom whom Dr. Vincent of Chautauqua pinned down "at some point between Chicago and St. Louis," [4] and engaged to teach Hebrew at the Institution.

Young Dr. Harper was an immediate success at Chautauqua. Evidently Dr. Vincent recognized in him the talent for organization and administration later to be demonstrated on a larger scale at Chicago, for in 1885 the prospectus for the summer term lists "William M. Harper [*sic*], Ph.D. Principal, Chautauqua School of Hebrew," and in 1887 he was made principal of the College of Liberal Arts, which position he held until 1898.

In his work as principal, Harper was placed in a close working relationship with Dr. Vincent, and in this association he undoubtedly felt the passionate force of Vincent's ideas concerning the role and mission of the higher education, ideas which Harper himself was later to share. In language which was for him extravagant, Vincent devoted many lines in the *Chautauquan* to eulogies of college life. In the issue for March, 1885, he discussed at length seven benefits of college training: the act of leaving home for a specific purpose; discipline in the "enforced system"; associations with fellow students, which "stimulate" the best elements in a man; "associations with professors and tutors (sometimes of little value)"; "mental discipline," which endows the student with "power to observe with scientific exactness, to generalize wisely from accumulated data, to project hypotheses"; "the comprehensive survey of the universe"; and finally, "self discovery."

> College life is the whole of life packed into a brief period, with the elements that make life magnified and intensified, so that tests of character may easily be made. It is a laboratory of experiment, where natural laws and conditions are pressed into rapid though normal operation, and processes otherwise extending over long periods of time are crowded to speedy consummation. Twenty years of ordinary life, so far as they constitute a testing period of character, are by college life crowded into four years.
>
> Arguments should be used, appeals made, assistance proffered, that a larger percentage of American youth may aspire after college privileges. . . .
>
> Chautauqua lifts up her voice in favor of liberal education for a larger number of people. She would pack existing institutions until wings must be added to old buildings, and new buildings put up to accommodate young men and maidens who are determined to be educated.
>
> Chautauqua would exalt the profession of teacher until the highest genius, the richest scholarship, and the broadest manhood and womanhood of the nation would be consecrated to this service.
>
> Chautauqua would give munificent salaries and put a premium on merit, sense, fact and culture in the teacher's office.
>
> [Chautauqua] . . . is as I have elsewhere said, a John the Baptist, preparing the way for seminary and university.

Dr. Harper's enthusiasm for new ideas was never difficult to awaken, and his optimistic nature must have thrilled to the vision that Vincent created of crowded, bustling colleges, eager students, and honored faculty members. It was a vision which Harper never forgot and which he tried desperately to realize at Chicago. The crowds of earnest students of all ages that invaded Chautauqua each summer or engaged in winter correspondence study convinced him that there existed in America a great multitude who thirsted after knowledge as an end in itself. Chautauqua stood ready to supply this need. Registrar Holmes wrote: "We appeal to a vast, an eager and earnest constituency. To know, only to know, is the earnest cry of multitudes of our fellows." [5]

Chautauqua leaders were insistent, however, that Chautauqua's work in secular education was only temporary:

> We expect that the work of Chautauqua University will be to arouse so much interest in the subject of general liberal education that by and by in all quarters young men and women will be seeking means to obtain such education in established resident institutions. [6]
>
> The plans so far described can not, in conformity with conventional ideas or with the best standards, be called higher education. They promote the interest of the higher education to say the least, but should neither be over-valued nor under-estimated.
>
> . . . colleges and universities generally, may eventually relieve Chautauqua from this responsible work, fraught with danger of misconstruction and misrepresentation. [7]

They emphasized, too, that the "credits" earned by students through their reading courses were not to be confused with college credits:

> A C. L. S. C. diploma, although radiant with thirty-one seals— shields, stars, octagons,—would not stand for much at Heidelberg, Oxford, or Harvard . . . an American curiosity . . . it would be respected not as conferring honor upon its holder, but as indicating a popular movement in favor of higher education. [8]

These ideas concerning the transcendent importance of higher education, together with the modesty of the Chautauqua officials concerning the efforts of their own institution, probably gave Harper food for thought. He was engaged in teaching Hebrew by correspondence and he had no personal contact with his correspondence students. Chautauqua's system provided for intensive contact between instructor and pupil during the summer as well as communication by mail during the rest of the year, yet Chautauqua leaders felt that their institution was only a way station in America's progress to something higher. Harper had seen the crowds that flocked to Chautauqua and he felt their passionate enthusiasm for learning. He found men, women, and children of all ages anxious to increase their store of knowledge and appreciations in areas other than his beloved Hebrew. He had been given an assignment, as principal of the Liberal Arts College, that carried with it the responsibility for securing fifteen department heads and one hundred or more teachers, preparing sections for over two thousand students, planning a curriculum to include language and literature, mathematics and science, music, art, physical culture and practical art. He had the task of editing the catalogue, planning and supervising the publicity, and securing approximately three hundred "events" (lectures, sermons, entertainment) for each session. He was expected to take an active part in helping to formulate the policies of the Institute itself, with Dr. Vincent, Mr. R. S. Holmes, the registrar, and other top-level administrators. He was forced, in a relatively short space of time, to organize his ideas about the function of education into a consistent whole, to adapt and modify his own theories to fit the needs of Chautauqua, and to assimilate into his own thinking the experience of the Chautauqua leaders. In so doing, he had discovered new devices in teaching and administration because he was forced to in order to meet the exigencies of the situation in which he found himself. No doubt he felt himself hardened and purified by the responsibilities and pressures to which he had been subjected, and he may have drawn a conclusion from this experience that helped him to generalize that survival was for those individuals or institutions that adjust to changing conditions.[9]

Meanwhile, in spite of the load he was carrying at Chautauqua and at Morgan Park, he continued to write and to publish. He had already brought out four textbooks: *The Elements of Hebrew* and *Hebrew Vocabularies* in 1881, and *Lessons of the Intermediate Course* and *Lessons of the Progressive Course* in 1882. In 1883, the year he joined Chautauqua, he had published a *Hebrew Manual* and *Lessons of the Elementary Course,* and in 1885, the year he was made a principal at Chautauqua, he completed and had published his *Introductory Hebrew Method and Manual.*

The latent passion for systematic organization that Harper possessed was undoubtedly stimulated by his Chautauqua experience. Perhaps his encounter with the "system of correspondence with professors of departments" that Chautaqua had begun in 1878 prompted him to undertake something similar at Morgan Park, although Hulbert attributes his inspiration to a different source:

> He saw somewhere a notice to the effect that some rabbi proposed to teach Hebrew by correspondence. Forthwith, with an electric pen, he drew up a series of lessons, and importuned the ministers whom he knew to begin or review their Hebrew. The next year the lesson-slips were printed, and names and addresses of clergymen of the various denominations were gleaned from the ecclesiastical yearbooks, and alluring circulars were sent broadcast over the land inviting to the study or restudy of the language of the Old Testament. . . . The expanding work crowded him out of his private library into

larger quarters, and thence into a vacant store which he rented in the village. There fonts of Hebrew type and outfits for compositors, bookkeepers and proofreaders, lesson correctors and business exploiters, were installed; and the village postmaster attained a higher postal rank by reason of increasing traffic and the sale of stamps.[10]

Next, he decided he needed two more things: journals to offer media for communication between students and scholars, and jobs for those of his students who successfully completed his courses of instruction.

The first need was supplied by the launching of *The Hebrew Student,* designed to appeal to the less scholarly, and *Hebraica,* a journal whose pages would be devoted to the more technical aspects of Hebrew study.

The second was not solved in any significant degree in spite of his efforts. Hulbert writes, somewhat acidly, it would seem:

> To round out the great endeavor and make it in every way complete one thing more was needed. With the machinery for making trained Hebraists running smoothly and successfully, its originator plainly foresaw that a market for the finished product must be created. He thereupon evolved the idea of establishing Hebrew and Bible chairs in all the colleges of the land; and to his aspiring pupils there came in consequence the alluring vision of useful and lucrative positions. It would seem that Christian colleges, glorying in the Bible as their very cornerstone, could not be induced to put Hebrew on a par with Greek and Latin, nor to raise the Sacred Scriptures to the same dignity with the pagan classics; and it would also seem that the students in training for these college chairs, soon to be established, had to content themselves for the most part with plain country parsonages.[11]

During these years, Harper devised a method for financing his enterprises that was quite in keeping with the spirit of his time, and at the same time characteristic of the man himself. He established a joint stock company, and offered shares at one hundred dollars each, the proceeds to be used to support the correspondence school venture and the journals until they should become self supporting. His innate optimism led him to believe that this was a sound financial venture. Dr. T. W. Goodspeed, secretary of the Baptist Union Theological Seminary, wrote: "He himself was so impressed by the interest manifested in his work that he believed he could make the stock pay dividends to the investors, and toiled unremittingly to realize his hopes." [12]

It was natural that such an outstanding young Baptist should have been known, by reputation at least, to the leading Baptist layman in the United States, John D. Rockefeller, Sr. Mr. Rockefeller, a devout man (although portrayed by many press cartoonists as a monster of greed), was generous if cautious in his contributions to his denomination. His experience had undoubtedly taught him that money was of little avail in any enterprise if good men were lacking, and apparently he was convinced that this young Dr. Harper was a good man. On April 5, 1886, he found time to write Dr. Goodspeed, informing him that Yale had designs on Dr. Harper.

The possibility that Harper might be lured away added to the gloom already existing at Morgan Park over the collapse of the University of Chicago, sister institution to the Seminary in the eyes of many Baptists. Founded in 1856, the year of Harper's birth, the "old" University, as it came to be called, opened its doors in 1857. Its president, the Reverend Dr. Galusha Anderson, was unable to prevent the Mutual Union Life Insurance Company from seizing the property under foreclosure proceedings, and the Baptist ministers of Chicago, in their regular weekly meeting, regretfully advised the trustees to allow the foreclosure to go uncontested.

A possible solution of both difficulties, however, had occurred to Dr. Goodspeed:

> We have proposed to Dr. Harper to assume the presidency of our wrecked and ruined University and re-establish it here at Morgan Park, retaining the oversight of the Department of Hebrew in the Seminary. The suggestion has taken a strong hold on him and if he had some assurance of help, he would not hesitate to do it.[13]

Support for this scheme was not forthcoming, however, from Rockefeller's quarter: "I really do not know what to say about the University," he wrote. "I realize it is desirable, very, for the Seminary to have it continued." If, he went on to say, an increase in salary would hold Harper, he would be willing to make a commitment for that purpose.

Since Harper was leaving for an interview at New Haven, Goodspeed proposed to Rockefeller that Harper call on him in New York, ostensibly to explain to him that newspaper reports of Rockefeller's intention to give two hundred thousand dollars to resuscitate the "old" University were not emanating from Morgan Park.

On April 26, 1886, in New York City, Dr. Harper met John D. Rockefeller for the first time, and he probably then introduced the subject of the University of Chicago, if only to exonerate his friends from rumor-mongering. With characteristic caution, Mr. Rockefeller no doubt kept the conversation on what was for him safe ground; in his reply to Goodspeed he wrote: "I said all I could with a view to having him remain with us, and shall regret much if he does not, but I fear he will not."

Dr. Harper did not. He became a member of the faculty of the Divinity School at Yale. He did not, however, sever all connections with the institution at Morgan Park but planned to spend the month of January each year teaching at the Seminary. On May 12, 1886, Dr. Ira M. Price was engaged as instructor in Hebrew to take Harper's place.

The year 1886 closed without any real progress being made toward interesting Mr. Rockefeller in the Chicago scheme. Dr. Goodspeed considered a call to the presidency of Kalamazoo College, one of the less shaky Baptist colleges of the Midwest, but he refused it after receiving a gently reproving letter from Mr. Rockefeller.[14] Several times during that year Goodspeed ventured to interest Rockefeller in the progress, or lack of it, that the Chicago group was experiencing in trying to revive the university, but to no avail. Goodspeed had not given up hope, however. On September 17, 1886, he wrote Harper, ". . . hold yourself ready to return here some time as President of a new University."

Harper's return to Yale in the fall of 1886, as Divinity School professor of Semitic Languages, was a striking contrast to his first acquaintanceship with Yale College. He had then been a naïve young graduate of a fresh-water college, only moderately well-prepared, probably overawed by the size and wealth of the Yale campus (Muskingum had only one building), and certainly younger (at seventeen) than most of Yale's freshmen. But now, a short thirteen years later, he was returning as a colleague of Professor William D. Whitney, who had taught him Sanskrit, and Professor George E. Day, of the "line of New England Hebraists who looked back to Moses Stuart as their head." [15] More than this, Harper was a well-known figure in his own right as principal of the

Chautauqua Liberal Arts College, at the time possibly the most widely publicized institution in the country.

No doubt the contrast with the Yale he had known in the seventies struck Harper also. Timothy Dwight had been chosen president by the Corporation in May, 1886, and had been inaugurated on July first of that year. In October, the same month that Harper took up his duties, the Corporation authorized the use of the title "University," and this change was legalized by an act of the Connecticut legislature, signed by the governor on March 8, 1887. A building program was under way; the number of graduate students had increased from 56 to 125; and in the first four years of President Dwight's administration, gifts to the institution had totaled $1,224,390, a phenomenal sum for those days.[16] Yale was on the march.

Harper's move from Morgan Park to New Haven necessitated finding a three-story house for the offices and printing shop connected with the Institute of Hebrew and the two journals, *Hebraica* and *The Hebrew Student*. By this time his entourage consisted of Dr. Robert F. Harper, his brother, who was assistant editor of *Hebraica;* George F. Goodspeed, assistant editor of *The Hebrew Student* (and nephew of T. W. Goodspeed of the Morgan Park faculty); Frank K. Saunders, who conducted the Correspondence School; and George E. Robertson, business agent. In addition to these key staff members, three stenographers, five correspondence instructors, three clerks, a bookkeeper, and a host of part-time students were employed.

Harper's teaching duties in his first year at Yale included eight hours of Hebrew, four of Assyrian, four of Arabic, and one each of Aramaic and Syriac. He had over fifty theological students who took one or more of these courses, plus seven graduate students. It might appear that all these commitments, plus the Chautauqua responsibility, would have left him little time for additional work, but he arranged for a series of public lectures on the English Bible in each of four communities—Brooklyn, Vassar, Boston, and New Haven—and he met these groups once each week in each city. Yet his students found no flagging in his energies. One of them wrote: "To us all his methods and his ambitions were a revelation, and his leadership was so inspiring that the hours of study which he demanded were given as a matter of course and with great heartiness."

Several incidents or events that occurred during the first two years of Harper's return to Yale make it appear likely that it was at this time that he turned his attention to research as an outlet for his talents and training in Semitic languages, as a teaching discipline, and as an activity that would result in a lasting contribution to human knowledge and welfare.

During his student days at Yale he had been told by Professor Whitney that there were great opportunities for an "up and coming" young man in Semitic scholarship. He had, however, demonstrated no interest in research as such; President Andrews had found him uninterested in the history and literature of the languages that he possessed. His work at Morgan Park and the early numbers of *Hebraica* show no indication of an interest in the "Higher Criticism," or indeed of any awareness of the contributions to archaeological or historical research possible to a man with a good knowledge of Semitic languages.

Soon after he came to Yale, however, Harper offered one nontechnical course to undergraduates, "Hebrew and Other

Semitic Literature." For the first time in his life, Harper was teaching undergraduates. He had taught academy boys at Granville (and had taught them Latin and Greek); theological students at Morgan Park whose interest in Hebrew was vocational; and adults at Chautauqua who were already motivated, for their own obscure reasons, to learn Hebrew. Never before had he faced a class of undergraduates whose main interest was in the cultural values to be derived from the study of Hebrew. Unlike theological students, they were not interested in simply learning to read the Bible in Hebrew; they wanted to know more about the Bible as an historical document.

Always a consummate teacher, Harper sensed what his class wanted. He sensed, too, that many other people wanted the same thing: to know how the Bible had been written, how much of it was to be accepted as God's word, and how much of it was "filler." They had heard some persons say that there was evidence to show Moses did not write all the Pentateuch, and they had heard those persons damned as heretics and worse by fundamentalist ministers. They wanted to know what a scholar thought about these questions, and Harper was prepared to tell them.

Harper owed much to Yale and, particularly, to President Timothy Dwight. It is unfortunate that several years later, when Harper announced his intention to resign, a coolness developed between the older and the younger man. In their subsequent writings no mention of the other appears. Events at this time, however, indicate that President Dwight was well disposed to Harper.

Before his election to the presidency, Dwight had held the New Testament Chair in the Divinity School, and it was natural that he should have followed with interest young Harper's success in awakening enthusiasm for Bible study. That he was impressed with Harper's work cannot be doubted, for not only did he secure for him a chair in the College, but he proposed to put him in charge of a graduate department that would apply the methods of German scholarship to linguistic study. Dwight has described this department as it later materialized without Harper:

> In the Department of Theology a number of optional courses were added to the required curriculum, in which what is called "the seminary method" of original research was adopted. With the advance of learning in all branches of professional study, the opportunities for the best and most remarkable education have been enlarged, and in no respect, perhaps, more than in the line of individual and independent investigation. . . . The development of the entire plan of the Graduate School has certainly been very remarkable . . . as well as the rapid progress in all lines of investigation.[17]

It is difficult at the present time to realize the high hopes that many academicians held for the painstaking methodology of German scholarship, particularly in the field of linguistics. The restrained prose of President Dwight's reminiscences does not convey the excitement felt by some of Harper's friends at the news of the proposal. One writes:

> Here you have a chance to throw the millions of Yale and all her prestige and power into the biggest and newest movement of the time—the Semitic—and to run it so as to stand at the head of the liberal-conservative school of scholarship, that will soon have answered the skepticism of Germany by utilizing the best and only permanent results of German scholarship.[18]

Harper's correspondent, and undoubtedly Harper himself, believed wholeheartedly in the validity of the Old Testament as an historical document. The German scholars who had used the tools of linguistic research on the scriptural texts had unfortunately succumbed to skepticism and the net result of their researches had weakened rather than strengthened the intellectual basis of revealed religion. The subject was a touchy one, but might it not be possible, in a department of theology, to keep a firm hold on faith and yet by a careful pruning of inconsistencies eventually uncover a firm intellectual basis for that faith? The idea certainly appealed in some measure to Harper, for although he did not take the proffered post, he prepared and published a series of articles in *Hebraica*, cast in the form of a debate with Professor William Henry Green, of Princeton, on "The Pentateuchal Question." Professor Green, firmly conservative, made no bones about labeling those who accepted the interpretation of the "Higher Criticism" (i.e., that the five books of the Pentateuch were written at different times, and by many different authors) as little better than atheists. Harper, although he did not identify himself with the conclusions of the critics, ably defended the approach and outlined the methods of the school of historical criticism.

This interest in historical criticism, which his contacts with the faculty at Yale during the regular academic year had developed, led Harper to try a similar approach at Chautauqua the following summer. The *Chautauquan* for May, 1888, carried the following announcement in the form of an advertisement:

July 5–26—*School of English Bible*

This department is designed to meet the increasing demand for a *more scholarly and critical study of the English Bible.* For three weeks some of the *best Biblical Specialists in the country* will give their energies to this work. The scope of the School is comprehensive; its plan is new. There ought to be five hundred earnest enthusiastic students in the department next summer.

There were five hundred students, so earnest and enthusiastic that in 1890 the term was extended from the original three weeks to six weeks. The project, and Harper, received some criticism from conservative sources, but both were ably defended by Bishop Vincent, Chautauqua's chancellor:

The issue raised is whether Dr. Harper and others believe in Moses as an author. They declare that they do so believe; and it is replied that what they have written is fatal to the Mosaic authorship of the first five books of the Bible. In short it has become a personal controversy and it ought to be put an end to, in that form of it, as soon as possible. If the higher critics are wrong, let it be clearly shown. The day is gone for settling questions by calling names. A rationalist who denies all inspiration is a very different person in faith and works from the Christian Scholars who are quite sure Moses did not write the account of his own death and are willing to inquire diligently into all matters pertaining to the authorship of the books of Moses.[19]

Harper was fortunate to have such a competent apologist; he was fortunate also to be able to bring so quickly into concrete existence at Chautauqua each summer the ideas that Yale gave him each winter. His work load was incredible, yet he never took what might be called a vacation. Yale claimed him from September to June, Chautauqua from June to September, and he drew inspiration from both.

Meanwhile, other advances were being made at Chautauqua, and Harper was playing an active part in the planning. According to Professor Herbert B. Adams, in an informative magazine article,[20] Dr. Vincent visited England in October,

1886. He was much impressed with the growth of the university extension movement there and immediately saw how Chautauqua might take the lead in a similar endeavor in the United States. "He wrote home to the Registrar of the Chautauqua College of Liberal Arts, and a conference was held with Dr. Harper, the principal, as early as November, 1886."

Harper was immediately drawn to the idea and it is easy to see why, for it appealed to his love for systematization and planning on the grand scale.

Mr. R. S. Holmes resigned as registrar at the January, 1888, meeting of the Board of Trustees of the Chautauqua Assembly in Buffalo, New York, but his successor, Professor W. D. McClintock, with Harper and the protagonists of the movement, applied himself toward university extension.

> The Registrar, Professor W. D. McClintock, shows that non-resident college work and the correspondence method are gaining favor in educational circles. . . . In this connection the Registrar points out the disadvantages under which the professors labor by reason of lack of opportunity to meet and consult, and also the need of funds to compensate teachers for doing the work properly. He recommends some plan by which a faculty may be provided, who shall give their whole time to this work. This part of the report was referred to a special committee to report at the next meeting.[21]

Apparently, however, no more than preliminary talks were possible until the summer of 1888, when a definite plan for Chautauqua University extension was drawn up by a committee consisting of Harper, Bishop Vincent and his son (George E. Vincent, director of the Chautauqua Press), Dr. Richard T. Ely, Professor Frederick Starr, and Professor H. B. Adams.

On September 15, 1888, "a small pamphlet setting forth the aims of 'Chautauqua University Extension' was issued, and circulated privately among those who would be most likely to be interested in the work." [22]

> The objects proposed were: (1) a revival in the United States of the original idea of a university as a voluntary association of students and itinerant lecturers for higher education by means of systematic courses of local lectures upon special subjects; (2) the promotion of good citizenship by the popular study of social science, economics, history, literature, political ethics, and the science of government, in continuous and progressive courses, under the guidance of competent teachers; (3) courses of instructive lectures upon natural science; (4) cooperation with American colleges and other institutions of learning in order to supplement their work by university extension courses; (5) affiliations with public libraries, mechanics institutes, lyceums, labor unions, guilds, young men's Christian Associations, Chautauqua Literary and Scientific Circles; (6) the higher education of the American people by the organization of the most intelligent and progressive local forces.

> The methods suggested were those of English university extension, comprising systematic lecture courses, a printed syllabus, class discussion, written exercises and final examination. . . . It was hoped that local branches of Chautauqua would prove instrumental in organizing local courses of extension lectures.[23]

The plan was formally announced for the summer of 1889:

> Chautauqua has led her patrons to expect a new development each year. She has not disappointed them in 1889. The University Extension Scheme has been launched, after more than a year's careful study and planning. This scheme proposes, in brief, to provide courses of lectures by university men on selected topics, the auditors to be given a syllabus with bibliography for each lecture and an examination to be given at the end to such as wish.[24]

University Extension at Chautauqua was an unqualified success. Within an incredibly short time, however, this and many other features of the Chautauqua movement were to be transferred to a larger arena. The question of the re-establishment of the "wrecked and ruined" old University at Chicago was not entirely dead, and several vigorous and tenacious persons were determined that it would revive, with William Rainey Harper as president.

William Rainey Harper

The Baptist Dream
of a Super-University

Of the Baptists who had as their goal the re-establishment of the "old" University of Chicago, the most persistent was Dr. T. W. Goodspeed, of the Morgan Park Seminary. He continued to discuss with Dr. P. S. Henson and Dr. Justin P. Smith, both Baptist clergymen of Chicago, various plans for the revival, but the root of their difficulties continued to be lack of funds, together with a scarcity of ideas as to how funds might be raised. Tantalizingly, they were all painfully aware that one man in the Baptist fold, John D. Rockefeller, possessed resources that would permit him to contribute lavishly to such a project, but Rockefeller seemed impervious to hints and suggestions.

In December, 1886, Goodspeed decided to take the bull by the horns. He wrote Rockefeller, asking permission to outline for him in detail the offers they had had at Morgan Park relating to re-establishing the University.[1] Rockefeller's reply was characteristic: "There is hardly a chance that I could give the least encouragement for assistance in respect to the University, but I will carefully read the communication you suggest."

Goodspeed persisted and enlisted the aid of Dr. Harper in his project. He wrote again to Rockefeller and arranged for Harper to write the financier, endorsing the proposals Goodspeed had made.

Mr. Rockefeller did not dismiss these letters as promptly as he had done Dr. Goodspeed's earlier importunings. Whether it was the firmer language of the later letters, the fact that Harper was now associated in the proposal, or merely the persistence shown by Goodspeed and his associates, Mr. Rockefeller decided to investigate further. He forwarded both letters to Dr. Augustus H. Strong, president of the Rochester Theological Seminary, with a covering note:

> I enclose herein a letter to me from Dr. Goodspeed dated January 7th and from Dr. Harper January 11th. I would be much obliged if you would, at a convenient time to you, say to me in confidence what you think of it.

There are several reasons why Mr. Rockefeller chose to get Dr. Strong's reaction at this time, for in addition to his denominational leadership and educational position, he had been a long-standing acquaintance, if not intimate friend, of the Rockefellers. Dr. Strong had held a pastorate in Cleveland at a time when Mr. Rockefeller was active in Baptist affairs, and other ties had also been formed.[2] The most important reason, however, was undoubtedly the fact that Dr. Strong was bursting with a plan of his own for an educational institution in New York City, a plan he had, at some previous time, communicated at least in brief to Rockefeller.

Strong quite naturally preferred his own plan. His reply

to Rockefeller took the form of a lengthy memorandum entitled, "A University: What It Is And Why We Need One." He believed New York was the most logical place for a Baptist university, and he outlined his reasons for thinking that the project should begin with an excellent school of theology. Academic departments could then be added, and students with goals other than the ministry could be admitted, but the whole institution would be pervaded by a teaching and a scholarship firmly and soundly rooted in Baptist theology.

This proposal to restore Theology to her former place as "queen of the sciences" is understandable as a reaction on the part of a devoutly religious man to the frankly secular influence of German university scholarship, which had already gained a firm foothold in the United States at the Johns Hopkins University. While far from Thomist, Strong's position does, in a sense, anticipate that of Robert M. Hutchins.

Perhaps Strong was impressed by reports of Harper's administrative skill, or perhaps he knew that Rockefeller held Harper in high regard; at any rate, Strong arranged to meet Harper in New York City in late September, 1887. Strong outlined his plan and Harper was intrigued. Strong reported to Rockefeller that

> Professor Harper agrees with me: if we begin now we can take the wind out of the sails of Yale, Harvard and even Johns Hopkins, whereas if we delay we lose the chances of prestige and success in being the first to initiate the idea of combining the broadest theological education with the beginning of a true University.

It is interesting to speculate concerning the effect such an institution might have had on the development of American higher education. Rockefeller was one of the wealthiest men in the country. Harper was to prove himself one of the most skilled of university administrators and Strong was undoubtedly one of the most competent theologians in the Baptist denomination. Working in concert, they might well have made such an institution successful. At that particular moment in history, the future direction of American higher education had not been determined. Johns Hopkins University, dedicated to the ideals of German scholarship, was off to a good start but had as yet few imitators. Harvard and Yale were now universities but in their faculties, the elite in prestige, pay, and promotion were teachers who appealed to philosophic principles rather than researchers primarily interested in facts. Cornell and the state universities were dedicated to service; Andrew D. White, Cornell's president, had written, in 1878, that he did not believe America could yet afford the luxury of "elegant learned investigations on points of mere scholarly interest." [3] A powerful university based on Strong's conception, vigorously supporting *a priori* reasoning, could have delayed and possibly diluted the acceptance of the research ideal in American higher education.

On October 29, 1887, Harper had an interview with Rockefeller and his report to Strong must have been favorable, for Strong replied: "It gratifies me exceedingly that you have received so much encouragement that such an institution may actually be established for our denomination in New York."

Shortly thereafter, however, Rockefeller became extremely busy. Perhaps the fact that the embargo of the Producers' Association of the Pennsylvania–New York oil fields went into effect on November 1, 1887, had something to do with his inaccessibility, but except for a brief note suggesting that Harper and he might "steal a few minutes for lunch together" there is no indication that Rockefeller made himself available for a second interview.

On November 26, 1887, Dr. Strong, who had grown restive, decided to write the financier "one more letter." It was henceforth the great regret of his life that he did so, although it is extremely doubtful whether his proposal could have succeeded with Mr. Rockefeller in any case, and even more doubtful that, in a matter affecting the welfare of his denomination, Mr. Rockefeller would have allowed himself to be influenced by personal considerations. It was Strong's misfortune to base his argument on Mr. Rockefeller's unpopularity, and to point out how, in his opinion, the oil man could secure the "favorable judgments" of the world at large by establishing "an institution for the public good —so great that it has manifestly cost a large self-sacrifice to build it."

Rockefeller's reply was prompt and terse. He wrote Dr. Harper on November 30:

> Yours, 29th at hand. I am also just in receipt of one from Dr. Strong, of the 26th, and have felt obliged to write him the following:
>
> *My dear Dr. Strong:*
> *For all of the reasons, I have decided to indefinitely postpone the question of a University or Theological Seminary in New York.*
> *Very truly yours,*
JOHN D. ROCKEFELLER
>
> I am just making preparation to leave the city, probably this afternoon, until next week.
> Yours very truly,
JOHN D. ROCKEFELLER

And so ended the vision of a great theologically-centered Baptist university in New York City. Could it have succeeded? If it had, Augustus Strong and not William Rainey Harper would have played the important role in shaping the future of American higher education, for Strong was the dominant member of this partnership. But now Harper's star was in the ascendancy.

Early in 1887, a proposal was made in the *Standard*, a Baptist weekly paper published in Chicago, for the formation of a general Baptist educational society to investigate and take steps to strengthen the Baptist colleges and universities in the United States, particularly west of the Alleghenies. The *Examiner*, a denominational journal published in New York, opposed the plan. A convention was held on May 16, 1887, in the Calvary Baptist Church in Washington, D.C., and Dr. Strong led a delegation from New York pledged to defeat the proposal. The convention voted, 188 to 24, to establish the American Baptist Educational Society with Francis Wayland, of Connecticut, as president and Frederic T. Gates, of Chicago, as corresponding secretary.

Frederic Gates was a curiously contradictory man, but perhaps no more so than Mr. Rockefeller himself. Allan Nevins characterizes him in these words:

> Devoutly religious he unquestionably was; but at heart he was a businessman, shrewd, alert, aggressive, and capable of driving hard bargains. The time was not far distant when this former minister, coming to New York, would essay to teach Wall Street itself some lessons, and would do it.[4]

Gates' combination of religious devotion and business acumen could be expected to appeal to Rockefeller, who possessed the same traits, and the two men were later to become more and more closely associated, Rockefeller eventually bringing Gates to New York City and entrusting him with all his philanthropies.

Gates undertook his duties as secretary of the newly formed American Baptist Educational Society with characteristic vigor and intelligence. He prepared a questionnaire and circulated it among leaders of the denomination. Assembling his data, he decided that what was necessary to the educational health of the denomination was a strong college at Chicago, and on October 15, 1888, he presented his findings in a paper which he read before a Baptist ministers' conference in Chicago.[5]

Two days before Gates read his paper, a momentous meeting took place between Harper and Rockefeller at Poughkeepsie. The meeting itself was not uncommon, since Mr. Rockefeller frequently attended the Sunday series of lectures that Dr. Harper was giving at Vassar College. On this particular Sunday, however, the conversation was hardly casual, and, even allowing for Harper's easily kindled enthusiasm, Rockefeller once and for all seemed to have made up his mind in favor of Chicago. Harper communicated the shift immediately to his friends in the Chicago camp:

> He stands ready after the holidays to do something for Chicago. It will have to be managed, however, very carefully; but the chief point of my letter is this: in our discussions of the general question he showed great interest in the Educational Society (I mean the new one) and above all talked for hours in reference to the scheme for establishing the great university at Chicago instead of in New York. This surprised me very much. As soon as I began to see how the matter struck him I pushed it and I lost no opportunity of emphasizing

this point. The long and short of it is I feel confident that his mind has turned, and that it is a possible thing to have the money which he proposed to spend in New York diverted to Chicago.

He himself made out a list of reasons why it would be better to go to Chicago than to remain in New York. Among other things the fact that there would be an entire uniformity of the thing, which could hardly be expected if the university were established in New York.

Following the denouement at Vassar, events moved with rapidity. Gates' "Need" was widely circulated among prominent Baptists, and received widespread approbation. His report was factual, containing data on endowments, enrollments, spheres of influence, numbers of books in libraries, and the like, in colleges operated under the aegis of the Baptist denomination. It compared the Baptist effort in higher education with that of other denominations—to the shame of the Baptists—and ended with a plan to found, in Chicago, "a great college, ultimately to be a university," with an endowment of several millions, a plant equal to any on the continent, a faculty

> giving the highest classical as well as scientific culture . . . and aiming to counteract the western tendency to a merely superficial and utilitarian education—an institution wholly under Baptist control as a chartered right, loyal to Christ and his church, employing none but Christians in every department of instruction, a school not only evangelical but evangelistic, seeking to bring every student into surrender to Jesus Christ as Lord.

Gates' report was a masterpiece. First, it was as seemingly incontrovertible as a balance sheet, and to a generation that was beginning to regard bank statements as partaking in some measure of Holy Writ, this was a decided asset. Next, it neatly piqued the Baptists in their denominational pride, and, last, it ended in a burst of familiar yet stirring Baptist fervor.

On the same day that Gates delivered his address to the ministers in Chicago, Dr. Goodspeed wrote Harper jubilantly:

> It is indeed just the decision to which so keen sighted and level headed a man as Mr. Rockefeller might be expected to come. The location of a great institution at Chicago would awaken no antagonism, would injure no other institution, would rather help all and would give something like unity to our entire denominational education system.

The following month Harper again saw Rockefeller at Vassar, and although the young professor might have feared that the financier's ardor had cooled, as it had done one year previously, his fears were soon dispelled. He wrote Goodspeed:

> I spent 10 hours yesterday with Mr. Rockefeller; he came to Poughkeepsie. The result of our interview was the telegram which I sent you last night. He is practically committed to the thing. The great plan which now lies open is (1) a college and university at Chicago; (2) a theological seminary of high grade in New York City; (3) the organization of colleges in the West. This is the way the thing presents itself to him and the order in which the things are to be done. He is very much in earnest or surely, he would not have come up to Poughkeepsie. He had not read Gates' paper but I gave him the substance and it fired him up. President Taylor was with me in the greatest part of the interview and backed up everything I said. He is a strong ally.

Plans, or at any rate proposals, for the new institution had progressed to the stage where the principals had begun to talk figures. Goodspeed felt the time was ripe to propose financial terms; accordingly, he suggested a goal of four million dollars, Mr. Rockefeller to start the ball rolling with one and a half millions, then to pay the lion's share of the balance.

Gates had several conferences with Rockefeller, and as a result of these he proposed to the financier that he be empowered to solicit a committee of nine prominent men [6] who were to study the situation, visit Chicago, and make a report on their findings. This arrangement was carried out; thus, when Gates was called to New York by Rockefeller just prior to the May meeting of the American Baptist Education Society, he was well fortified with a collective statement of opinion by men whose judgment he knew Rockefeller respected. Before he left New York he had Rockefeller's pledge of $600,000, contingent upon the condition (among others) that "the whole sum of one million dollars be subscribed before June 1, 1890."

The Society met in Tremont Temple, Boston, May 18, 1889. Gates was instructed to withhold the announcement of the oil king's gift until the matter of the Chicago site had been thoroughly debated. But all was harmony. Dr. Strong arose to state that God had reversed his (Strong's) opinion on the matter of the Chicago institution, and he thereupon gave his blessing to the enterprise. The vote was unanimous in favor of establishing a Baptist college at Chicago. The announcement of Rockefeller's gift brought a salvo of applause and cheers. The session ended in an excess of good feeling. Now all that remained was the raising of $400,000.

To Goodspeed, the task seemed hopeless. He had been

vainly attempting to raise a smaller sum, and he knew, or thought he knew, the apathy of Chicagoans. But he had a powerful ally in Gates. That gentleman had already discovered those rules that he was later to formulate for the use of other fund-raisers. He knew, too, the uses of publicity and the wisdom of framing one's appeal on as broad a base as possible. Accordingly, the resolutions and other information about the project were "published . . . in the secular and religious press of Chicago, they were embodied in circulars and scattered in the pews of the churches, or sent broadcast by mail over the land." [7] Mr. Gates did not need to learn that the majority of donors of large gifts want to be sure that others beside themselves know of the cause and think it worthwhile. Mr. Gates could be quite cynical about philanthropy. He advised: "Appeal only to the nobler motives. His own mind will suggest to him the lower and selfish ones." The funds were slow in coming, but thanks largely to his own energy, persistence, and ingenuity, Gates was able to announce on May 27, 1890, to the third meeting of the American Baptist Education Society, that pledges amounting to $549,000, including a suitable tract of land donated by Marshall Field, had been acquired by the executive committee, and that therefore Mr. Rockefeller's pledge was redeemed.

Meanwhile, a serious hitch had developed in the plans. Dr. Harper seemed uninterested in accepting the presidency. Undoubtedly there were several reasons for this attitude. The Yale administration strenuously opposed any idea of Harper's leaving; Harper himself feared that he might lose his opportunity for contributions to Hebrew scholarship, and he was aware of his differences with the strict fundamentalists in his denomination. More important, his association with Dr. Strong had opened a new vista to him. He was no longer happy or satisfied, as he would have been in 1886, to become president of a college—even a "million dollar" college. He dreamed of a great university. In July he wrote Gates, "There must in some way be an additional million," and Gates went to work on Rockefeller. The outcome was an eight-point agreement, a *quid pro quo* in which the financier bound himself to an additional million. Harper notified Goodspeed of the new arrangement early in September and in return received a congratulatory message (which might be true): "It is a glorious thing you have accomplished, enough to make your life tell powerfully on our country and the world for all time." But, as usual, the good Dr. Goodspeed was worried. He wrote:

> I shall be surprised if the main objections and difficulties do not come from the Seminary board. Think it all over. Learn just the relation of the Yale Divinity School to the University Corporation. I see that its endowment funds are separate. I am going to write to several Universities having theological departments to learn the relations between them.

Although he had not yet been elected by the trustees (and, indeed, he was to deliberate many months before accepting), Harper began at once to act like a president, assigning certain tasks to Goodspeed and suggesting that he ". . . consider how money is to be obtained for the Theological building, which must begin at once in order that the Theological Seminary can be moved into the city within a year."

To others among his friends, however, he was more circumspect. To Dr. Morehouse in New York he wrote:

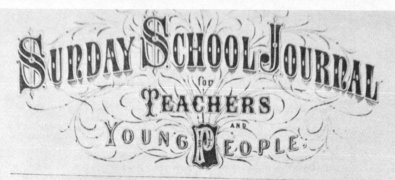

SUNDAY SCHOOL JOURNAL
for TEACHERS and YOUNG PEOPLE

CHAUTAUQUA EXTRA.

CHAUTAUQUA LAKE.

THE FEAST OF TABERNACLES.
August 4–18, 1874.
A WELCOME TO CHAUTAUQUA.
BY JOSEPHINE POLLARD.

We gather here, a pilgrim band,
 Whose home is set above,
And ere we reach the promised land,
 Prepare a feast of love.
Then welcome, welcome every one
 To scenes serenely bright,
Where Christ is our unclouded sun,
 And in his praise unite.

The morning dews—the fragrant breeze—
 The peaceful nights and days—
The smiling lake—the waving trees—
 Forever speak His praise.
Then welcome, welcome to the place
 Where hearts in love unite;
Where we behold a Saviour's face,
 And feel the saint's delight.

Miller's *Sunday School Journal*, inviting his readers to the first Chautauqua Assembly in 1874.

Dr. Vincent's handwritten description of the project, with Lewis Miller upper left and John H. Vincent upper right. The two men were co-founders of the Chautauqua Assemblies.

TEST QUESTIONS

For the Final Examination at the

CHAUTAUQUA LAKE,

August, 1874.

———•••———

1. Suppose you were asked by a pupil why you believe the Bible to be the word of God, what answer would you give?

2. Name the four classes in which the books of the Old Testament are usually arranged.

3. Name the minor prophets.

4. Name the three classes in which the books of the New Testament are arranged.

5. In what languages was the Bible originally written.

6. Describe the spirit in which the Sunday School teacher should study the word of God.

7. What should the Sunday School Teacher do with difficulties in the Bible which he can not understand or explain?

———0———

8. What is the object of the Sunday School?

9. Name the list of officers in a good Sunday School.

10. What is the relation of the Sunday School to the Church?

11. State FIVE duties which a Sunday School teacher owes to his scholars in school.

12. State FIVE duties which he owes to his scholar out of Sunday School.

13. Give FIVE short rules for a teacher in the preparation of his Sunday School lesson.

14. What are the various methods by which a teacher may use to the best advantage the EYES of his pupils?

15. What do you understand by TACT in teaching?

16. State your rules for getting your class interested in the lesson.

17. Why should the memorizing of Scripture be encouraged among our youth?

18. Why is home the best place to teach religion?

19. How may the Sunday School help home in its work?

20. How may our homes help the Sunday School?

21. Why should children attend the preaching service?

22. Why should older people attend the Sunday School?

On the conclusion of the first Assembly graduates were asked to answer these questions correctly.

Lake steamboats ran to the Fair Point wharf from both Jamestown and Mayville, N. Y. The stern-wheeler "Jamestown," shown here, carried over 3,000 passengers in 1875, when Ulysses S. Grant visited Chautauqua.

Named "The Ark," this wood-and-canvas building housed the first Chautauqua faculty. A pun of the period referred to it as "Knower's Ark."

The auditorium was out-doors; the gate (*above*) was the formal entrance to the grounds, which held a grove and fountain, shown below.

Wooden boardinghouses took care of the growing summer crowds.

The covered amphitheatre that replaced the outdoor auditorium was jammed with thousands of Chautauquans.

Outdoors, children played around the mound that depicted the Mount of Olives.

Swimming in Lake Chautauqua was one of the diversions. This is a 1908 picture.

In the nineties the police force for Chautauqua was known as the Department of Order. The chief wears the Dundreary whiskers.

Chautauqua from the steamboat landing (*c.* 1898).

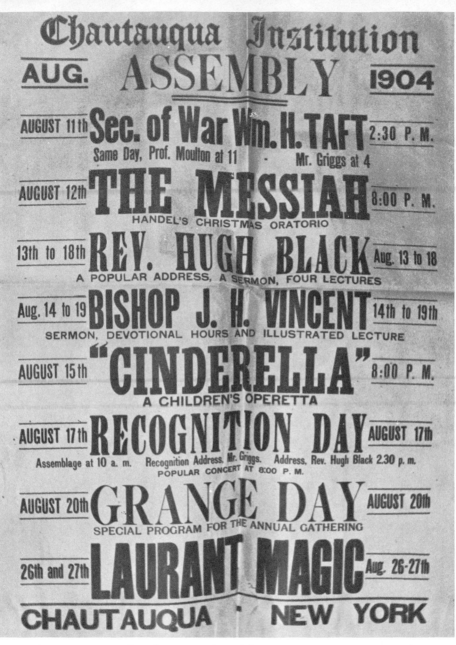

A 1904 poster for August, advertising the month's attractions.

Croquet was a favorite sport in the nineties, shown here played on a concrete surface. Amos Alonzo Stagg, world-famous coach, is shown below (lower left, in a striped blazer), photographed at Chautauqua in 1891, the year he joined the staff of the new University of Chicago as head coach. He was director of Chautauqua's athletic program from 1888 to 1896.

A class in Library Science, 1904. Melvil Dewey, in charge, worked out his famed decimal classification system while at Chautauqua.

A complete model of Jerusalem was part of the Bible lessons from the beginning.

John D. Rockefeller and William Rainey Harper at the Decennial Celebration of the University of Chicago, June 10, 1901.

. . . there is many a slip " 'twixt the cup and the lip" and so I do not think I am yet "in for the presidency." There are a good many details to arrange or I shall not see my way clear. I wish you would try your hand on a scheme for the combination of the Seminary and the University. This is going to be one of the hard problems.[8]

Harper was to have many "hard problems" that fall. In Chicago, however, events were proceeding with smoothness. Articles of incorporation having been filed, the University received its charter from the State of Illinois on September 10, 1890. A meeting of the Board of Trustees was scheduled for September 18, and a letter from Mr. Rockefeller, dated September 16, was read, announcing his million-dollar gift. At the same meeting, the committee on nominating a president reported, "recommending the selection of Professor William Rainey Harper, of Yale University." The report was unanimously and enthusiastically adopted by a rising vote, and a committee was selected to inform Dr. Harper and present him to the board. On entering, Harper expressed his appreciation of the honor conferred, and asked for six months time for consideration of the important offer.

At this point, Harper would seem to have achieved everything for which he had planned. He was president-elect of the new institution; he was guaranteed funds; he had a department of Semitic languages; seemingly, he had carte blanche. Yet once again he was to exhibit that curious reluctance to cut completely free that characterized his departure from Denison and Morgan Park. After an initial burst of enthusiasm for his "new plan," [9] he settled into a period of despondency. Goodspeed's letters to Harper during October bear evidence of this—they are sympathetic and encouraging. Harper, however, gave no clue at this time as to the real source of his agitation. He roused himself sufficiently during the first part of October to complain to the editor of the *Examiner* that his publicity was not satisfactory, and again on the twenty-first to invite Amos Alonzo Stagg, of Springfield, to confer with him to discuss "an important matter." The important matter was the organization of athletics at Chicago under Stagg, who (with Heffelfinger) was America's best-known college athlete. Harper's idea concerning Stagg was popular with Goodspeed, who wrote in response to a November 1 letter from Harper: "I am delighted with your suggestion about Stagg. He would be a great card."

But Harper's worry and agitation continued and finally became unbearable. Early in November, he wired Goodspeed and Gates to come to him in New Haven. There he laid before them his reservations concerning his fitness, in view of his association in the minds of many with the Higher Criticism, to be president of a Baptist university and school of theology. They, of course, reasured him, and all seemed well.

There was but a temporary lull, however. Harper's despondency grew with the weeks. His letters to Dr. Goodspeed finally upset that staunch supporter, and we find him writing Harper after the holidays:

> I hope if you were not frank with us at Dr. Northrup's at the meeting in September you will be now. . . . You should know by this time that I abhor destructive biblical criticism. It seems to me the poorest business any human being can engage in. I would rather shovel dung.
>
> I cannot suppose that this is the sort of thing you refer to or contemplate doing.

Possibly on the basis of this letter, possibly as a result of Dr. Northrup's advice, Harper felt it necessary to write Mr.

Rockefeller, tracing the reasons for his hesitation in accepting the presidency.

> I wrote to Dr. Northrup in September asking him to convene the gentlemen intimately connected with the Seminary in order that I might lay before them the exact facts of my belief. . . . As all agreed, my positions were largely different from those held by the rank and file of the denomination. They were, however, agreed also that on the essentials I was sound and that, therefore, there was no good reason why I should not accept the Presidency of the Seminary as well as the University. . . . I therefore propose to you that you select three or four gentlemen, e.g., Dr. Morehouse, Dr. Rhoades, Mr. Faunce; and that you give me the opportunity of laying before you and before them the exact facts, in order that (1) I may know whether I shall have the privilege of teaching my views in the University of Chicago, and (2) I may decide in case this privilege is not granted me, whether under all the circumstances, it is wise for the University and for myself to accept the position.[10]

Rockefeller did not wish to arbitrate questions of theology or sit in judgment upon Harper. He had already done so, privately, when he sought him out for the presidency of the new institution. Quite understandably, he allowed him to dangle for nearly a month while he framed a reply. When the suspense became too great, Harper wrote to Rockefeller: "I suppose I must resign my work here this week; the present situation seems to place me in a wrong light with the gentlemen of the faculty."

Harper then received two letters from Morehouse, dated January 31 and February 2. The first, urging him to take the bull by the horns and accept the Chicago presidency, was curt but explicit:

> Mr. Rockefeller has neither the time nor the inclination to decide mooted theological questions and to assume the responsibility

of saying what you teach—especially when that responsibility rests elsewhere. . . . The private commital has been made and the chief patron of the enterprise is not prepared to give his consent to a re-opening of the question or a reversal of the decision.

The astringent effect of this letter was exactly what Harper needed. On February 5 he presented his resignation to President Dwight, and eleven days later formally accepted the presidency of the University of Chicago.

Chautauqua Goes to Chicago

On my way home from Chicago the whole thing outlined itself in my mind and I have a plan which is at the same time unique and comprehensive, which I am persuaded will revolutionize university study in this country . . .[1]

Harper's plan to revolutionize university study first saw the light of day in a series of bulletins published in 1891 by the trustees of the University of Chicago. The first of these, *Official Bulletin No. 1*, appeared in January.

As Harper outlined his program in this first *Bulletin*, the university was to be divided into three parts: The University Proper, University Extension, and University Publication. The addition of the last two functions to the traditional role of a university was unquestionably a startling departure, and their admission to equality with the older disciplines was even more radical. But Harper had just begun. The University Proper, the *Bulletin* stated, would include:

1. *Academies.* [The first academy was to be at Morgan Park, Ill. Others were to be organized or affiliated "as rapidly as favorable opportunities are presented."[2]]

2. *Colleges.* [Here he would have four for undergraduate instruction: Liberal Arts, Science, Literature, and "Practical Arts," the last three granting the B.S. degree and the first, the A.B.]

3. *Affiliated Colleges.* [A system was to be worked out for the University to control in some measure the academic standards of independent institutions on the basis of voluntary association.]

4. *Schools.* [Projected were the Graduate School and, of course, the Divinity School, this last subject to an agreement which still remained to be worked out. At an unspecified future date professional schools of law, medicine, engineering, pedagogy, fine art, and music were to be established.]

5. *University Extension Work.* [To include lectures, evening courses, corresponding courses, special courses (in scientific study of the Bible), and library extension.]

6. *University Publication Work.* [To include the printing and publishing of university bulletins, catalogues, special papers, journals, reviews, books, "and the collecting by way of exchange, of papers, journals, reviews and books similar to those published by the University." [3]]

The most startling of the departures from orthodoxy were contained under the rubric "General Regulations." There were to be four "quarters" of instruction, beginning on the first of October, January, April, and July; each quarter would be divided equally into two terms of six weeks each, making it theoretically possible for a student to enter or graduate on any one of eight dates during the regular school year. Students were to pursue only two courses of study in any term: a "major" subject approximating twelve hours of classroom work each week, and a "minor" subject of approximately six hours. A student in continuous attendance might hope to graduate in three rather than four years, or he might take his course of study interspersed with periods of work and lasting much longer than the conventional four years.

Harper lists, in his first *Bulletin,* a number of advantages that might be expected to attend his reform. He believed his system would:

Provide for concentration rather than diffusion of energy, and for a flexible admissions and promotion schedule.

Furnish more stimulus and incentive toward original investigation.

Afford students an opportunity to take practical subjects such as book-keeping, stenography, etc., as well as the regular subjects.

Secure more intimacy between instructor and student.

Provide against instructors teaching "too many" subjects all at the same time.

Avoid the necessity of retaining unfit instructors.[4]

Make it possible for the university to attract outstanding professors for the summer quarter from other institutions.

Provide for the use of the University "plant" throughout the entire year.

Provide an opportunity for teachers, ministers and "professors in smaller institutions" to "avail themselves of the opportunity for University residence" [in the summer quarter].

Four more bulletins were published in the following months, but the greatest amount of care was apparently lavished on the preparation of *Bulletin No. 6,* in many ways the capstone of President Harper's plan for the University. The bulletin is entitled "The University Extension Division," and it is, fittingly, the first of the bulletins to bear the imprint "University of Chicago Press." Like the Press, it was designed, in Harper's words, "to bring the University into direct contact with human life and activity."[5]

Harper would distinguish University Extension from the University Proper in just one way—work done in the University Proper was work done in residence. In all other respects the work of the two divisions was identical, since University Extension was to be an organic part of the University.

The Division of University Extension was to have six departments. These were to be:

1. *Lecture-Study*

   This department was to conduct lecture-studies in courses of six or twelve weeks, usually one lecture per week. The lectures were to be units in themselves, and were to be supplemented by "syllabi, conversational classes, exercises and examination, given at points more or less distant from Chicago."

   Certificates could be earned, and credit toward a degree to the amount equal to that earned in residence might be secured through these courses. Three such courses would be considered equivalent to a *major*.

2. *Class Work*

   This was to be regular study in University courses, less concentrated and therefore distributed over a longer period. The unit course would equal a *major*. Examinations were to be taken on the University campus by those persons who wished credit toward a degree, and classes, according to demand, were to be organized paralleling, in content and method, those listed in the calendar of the University proper. Classes were to be organized mainly in Chicago and its environs. Fifty per cent of the credit toward an undergraduate degree might be earned in these classes. Graduate work in the Class-Work department could not exceed one-half the work done in residence.

3. *Correspondence-Teaching*

   The student registered in the Correspondence-Teaching department was to mail to the instructor each week an examination paper upon which he had written out the tasks assigned. The paper was to be corrected and returned to him with suggestions and criticism.

   Forty written recitations were to constitute a *major*, twenty

a *minor*, equivalent to the *majors* and *minors* on the University campus. The amount of undergraduate work done by correspondence could equal the amount done in residence toward a degree. For graduate work, the amount of correspondence work could not exceed one-half the residence work. Tuition was to be twelve dollars for a major, six for a minor.

4. *The Examination Department*

This department was to have responsibility for the examinations by which the granting of credit was determined in Lecture-Studies. It would also arrange on-campus examinations, to be given by the university Examiner, for those students in the Class-Study department who desired to take them. An interesting tieup with Affiliation is indicated in that all local examinations for accrediting the work of individuals, schools, and colleges was to be arranged by this department.

5. *The Library and Publication Department*

This department was to arrange small collections which would accompany those instructors in the Lecture-Study department, and prepare other collections to be made available to the classes, individual students, colleges, high schools, and normal schools.

A book-exchange, or, in Harper's term, a "book-clearing house," was to be set up for the use of libraries and individuals, to promote the exchange of volumes no longer needed.

The department was also responsible for preparing manuals, syllabi, pamphlets, and an official organ called the *University Extension Gazette*, to be edited by the Director.

6. *The Department of District Organization and Training*

This department was expected to coordinate within districts or areas the work of all the other departments of the division in that district, to organize clubs of students, distribute pamphlets, arrange meetings and conferences, and in general "to promote the interests of higher education."

Secondly, it was to recruit, train, and place organizers for the various functions of the Division, and to train lecturers and instructors for the proper conduct of their work in the Division.

When we compare the organizational scheme of the University of Chicago, as outlined in the *Bulletins,* with what had already developed at Chautauqua, the similarities are far beyond the possibility of mere coincidence. In 1885, six years before *Bulletin No. 1,* Vincent had proposed to his trustees the following organization:

    I. The Chautauqua Association
        a. The Summer meetings
        b. The Sunday School Normal Department
        c. The School of Languages
        d. The Chautauqua Teachers Retreat
    II. The Chautauqua Literary and Scientific Circles
    III. The Chautauqua School of Liberal Arts, now known as the Chautauqua University
    IV. The Chautauqua School of Theology
    V. The Chautauqua Press [6]

Compare this with the organizational scheme that Harper presented in *Official Bulletin No. 1:*

    I. The University Proper
        a. The Academies of the University
        b. The Colleges of the University
        c. The Graduate Schools of the University
        d. The Divinity Schools of the University
        e. Affiliated Colleges of the University
    II. The University Extension Work
        a. Regular courses of lecture
        b. Evening courses in university subjects
        c. Correspondence courses
        d. Special courses in a scientific study of the Bible
        e. Library Extension
    III. The University Press

The details of each plan of organization are more strikingly similar. For example, Harper's University Proper corresponds to the formally organized and accredited College of Liberal Arts, or "Chautauqua University," the difference being that the Chicago institution was to meet four times a year (in four assemblies, so to speak) and Chautauqua only once. The C.L.S.C. (Literary and Scientific Circles) had its counterpart at the new institution, as did the newly devised system of extension lectures under university auspices and for university credit. The plan for affiliation of colleges with Chicago may have had its inspiration from the many "little Chautauquas" that had sprung up all over the country, and which received much help from Vincent and his staff. As has been said, no formal relationship was cultivated between these "little Chautauquas" and the parent body, but the idea of such a relationship may well have appealed to Harper's passion for systematization.

Other similarities suggest themselves. Instead of regarding the summer quarter as an appendage to the regular college year, it is possible to regard the autumn, winter, and spring quarters as extensions of the Chautauqua idea: to offer four sessions rather than one. "Majors" and "minors" have their counterpart in the course work offered in the Chautauqua College of Liberal Arts, with its emphasis on intensive work during a relatively short period of time. The concept of the extension of university resources to everyone, regardless of age or academic preparation, was a Chautauqua idea, as was the proposal to allow work toward a degree to be distributed over a long period of time, or concentrated, or divided between work in residence and work by correspondence. Many of the

statements made by Registrar Holmes of Chautauqua in 1884 apply equally as well to Chicago:

> The Chautauqua University makes no limitation in the time allowed to students to complete her courses.
>
> The Chautauqua University does not require one who is enrolled as a student to take a complete course of study before giving official recognition to work already accomplished.

It is clear that, in the case of university extension, the idea was originally brought to Harper's serious attention as a result of Vincent's trip to England in the fall of 1886. The first *Official Bulletin* contained no mention of Lecture-Study under the heading University Extension,[7] but it was this particular phase of extension work that, during Harper's regime, was to receive the chief emphasis.[8]

In the considerable literature, both professional and popular, that greeted the founding of the University of Chicago, there is no mention of the similarity between the new institution and Chautauqua. This is more surprising when one considers the large number of professors—prolific writers, many of them—who offered courses at both institutions. These men ignored the organizational parallel, or perhaps they took it for granted.

Dr. Harper had every right, of course, to take the matured plan of Chautauqua, which had evolved over a fifteen-year period, and adapt it to fit the needs of formalized American higher education. He had played an important role in the evolution of that plan, and it is characteristic of him that he possessed both the vision to recognize its possibilities in a new situation and the skill and energy needed to realize those possibilities. Given his wholehearted acceptance of the Chau-

tauqua idea, it is difficult to see how he could have evolved another set of plans.

Perhaps the organizational parallels between Chautauqua and Chicago have been ignored because, although the two institutions looked similar on paper, they were actually quite different in outlook. One can trace Harper's emphasis on continuous sessions, concentrated doses of study, publication, correspondence work, lecture-study, and adult education to his connection with the Chautauqua movement. However, the articulation of these elements into a single plan for formal higher education, and his system for the administration of that plan, seem to be related less to his Chautauqua experience than to his belief that the advances made in his lifetime in the field of industrial organization should be applicable to higher education.

In his unpublished first report to the trustees, Harper states that the organization he designed "has more of the character of a Railroad Company or an Insurance Company than has heretofore characterized the organization of Universities and Colleges." No doubt he thought that, just as great combinations were demonstrating marvels of economy and efficiency in the industrial world, a well integrated and efficiently operated university might pioneer by using the same principles of combination and specialization in education.

Assuming that specialism is the order of the day, that competition is keen, and that "survival of the fittest" depends on the ability to adapt, that the weak will go under and the strong will take over their function, then is it not logical to conclude that a great university—given adequate resources and skillful leadership—should, by consolidating, and unifying, and "standardizing," perform in the sphere of education the same kind of efficient service that the great trusts, most particularly the Standard Oil Company, had performed in the sphere of industry?

Viewing the University within this frame of reference, many factors unite to form a consistent pattern. The administrative officers and their duties, as outlined by President Harper in *Official Bulletin No. 1*, are strikingly similar to those of a tightly knit, efficient industrial organization, consisting of (apart from the board of directors) the president, the cashier or treasurer, vice-president, works manager or plant director, and shop foremen.

> In other words, the work has been arranged on a business basis, with heads of departments who are held responsible. These heads, while frequently consulting with the President in reference to the particular work of their departments, have been given the largest possible freedom.[9]

This organization by departments, which Harper believed was "effected more rigidly than in any other institution," was termed by him "advantageous in that it located responsibility, drew sharp lines, and made more evident points of strength and weakness."

Instances of parallels between the organization and internal arrangements of the University and major business enterprises might be multiplied, some of them no doubt merely coincidental. The prestige enjoyed in the last decade of the nineteenth century by business and industrial leaders was real, however, and President Harper seems to have prided himself on adapting at least some of their methods of organization to his own problems. He was, of course, not alone in his admiration for industrial leaders, for they were real heroes to his generation. Walter Hines Page, editor and later wartime ambassador to Britain, wrote Harper in 1896:

> In spite of the impressiveness of the meeting at Buffalo, I was struck with the fact that there was not a single man nor woman there as far as I could find out, really of first-rate ability. I was talking about this to a group of very thoughtful men and women at Buffalo, and I will shock you by reporting what one of them said: "The truth is there are only three men of first-rate ability engaged in education in the United States, men, that is, as able as railroad presidents, or great manufacturers or great merchants." When the question was asked who these three men are, the speaker said, "Presidents Eliot, Harper and Jordan." [10]

Quite in keeping with the businesslike organization of the new university was the emphasis on production which was clearly stated in Harper's early plans.

> Promotion of younger men in the departments will depend more largely upon the results of their work as investigators than upon the efficiency of their teaching . . . . In other words, it is proposed to make the work of investigation primary, the work of giving instruction secondary.[11]

It should not be supposed that President Harper was alone, or even in the minority, in his stand on the importance of research to the exclusion of other interests in the university. In point of fact, several of the leaders in the higher education of his day went beyond him in their zeal. In this regard, two quotations from contemporaries are apropos, the first describing a kind of person who probably never really existed, but who has become part of our folklore:

> . . . in this function of truth-seeking by scientific research in every field of human knowledge, the university develops a very

peculiar and interesting kind of human being—the scientific specialist. The motives, hopes and aims of the investigator—I care not in what field of knowledge—are different from those of ordinary humanity. He must have a livelihood; but he is almost completely indifferent to money except as it secures simple livelihood and opportunity for his work. He is wholly indifferent to notoriety; he even shrinks from and abhors it; and his idea of fame is different from that of other men. He would indeed like not to have his name favorably known to millions of people, but to five or six students of the latin dative case, or of the greek particle . . . or of fossil beetles, or of meteorites or starfish. He much dislikes seeing his name in the newspaper; but he hopes that a hundred years hence some student of his specialty may read his name with gratitude in an ancient volume of the proceedings of some learned academy. . . . He is keen scented, devoted and enthusiastic, but for objects and ends so remote from ordinary topics that he rarely possesses what is called common sense. . . . A university should provide a large number of these specialists with a livelihood.[12]

This St. Francis of the laboratory would indeed have been an addition to any faculty and would have given his president not a moment's anxiety, with his shunning of the limelight in his quest for Greek particles or fossil beetles. Perhaps the layman's idea of a professor, for America, at least, was synthesized from such legends: the pathetic, shabby little figure who forgets his umbrella, to the amusement of his students, hardly to be taken seriously in the world of practical affairs.

G. Stanley Hall, like Eliot, was also confident that the new dispensation in American higher education was bringing forth a new kind of teacher, those "whose minds have got into independent motion; who are authorities, not echoes, who . . . live only for pure science and high scholarship,

and are not mere place holders or sterile routine pedagogues." [13]

Harper was determined that there should be no "sterile
routine pedagogues" at Chicago, and he regarded the graduate schools of his university as the capstone of his educational scheme. He considered all other educational institutions,
from the kindergarten through the college, and including
adult and correspondence courses, preliminary to these non-
professional or professional graduate schools, where the
approach to knowledge is that of the specialist or investigator. Those persons who did not reach this nirvana—and of
course the majority would not—would still have received
the best possible training since it would have been permeated with the "university spirit."

Harper never made it quite clear what he meant by the
"university spirit"; perhaps the term was sufficiently mean-
ingful to him so that to enlarge upon it seemed superfluous.
Apparently he meant a devotion to, or respect for, scientific
methods of acquiring data and testing hypotheses without
regard for preconceptions. Meanwhile, the great mass of
people who could never become researchers might still be
taught to wait patiently for a solution to their problems
until the state of exact scientific knowledge had progressed
to a point at which a solution could be scientifically demonstrated.

One other facet of Harper's plan for a university remains
to be considered, and that is its scope.

In the fall of 1887, when Dr. Strong, of the Rochester
Theological Seminary, first expounded his plan for a Baptist super-university to Dr. Harper, the latter came back in
a few weeks with a proposal to systematize and coordinate

all Baptist education in the United States. Strong protested that the time was not ripe for such a project and that it would become them to concentrate first on the New York institution. Harper subsided, and no more was heard about this project at the time. The idea seemingly never left him, however, for variations of it crop up many times in his published writings.

Two words are frequently used by Harper in these writings: "system" and "order." He never ceased to be upset and irritated by the formlessness and "chaos" of American education:

> It does not require the knowledge of an expert to see that, in this great multiplicity of plan and method, purpose and scope, there is no such thing as system. This work consists of a hundred thousand disconnected parts, without adjustment to each other and entirely devoid of relationship to any general scheme. These parts cannot be said to be even loosely connected. The same thing is repeated in a thousand ways; each way, however, being sufficiently distinct and different to make void every effort looking towards adjustment or connection. Germany may be said to have a system of education, France likewise; but in America, as a whole, there is no trace of anything that might rightly be called a system. . . . It is possible to go even farther and to say that there is no such thing as order. Whatever phase of this activity we study there is discovered chaos and confusion; no order or plan.[14]

> . . . The association of colleges may be either that of a state, as is already true of the State of New York, or that of a denomination (the bond in this case being very close) or that of a district, such as New England, or the Valley of the Mississippi. . . . The universities, supposing the number to be ten, fifteen or twenty, should, let me say, unite in a federation. . . . Through this federation of Universities will come the crowning feature of our American system—a National university.[15]

In another connection, some years later, he wrote:

> All this points to the development of a system of our higher educational work. The change of certain colleges into junior colleges, and of others into academies, the association of the colleges of a denomination or a geographical district with each other, and the close association of such colleges with the universities—all this will contribute toward a system of higher education (something which does not now exist in America), the lack of which is sadly felt in every sphere of educational activity. System means organization, and without organization, without the sharp distinctions and the recognized standards which come with organization, the work, however excellent, lacks that essential element which gives it the highest character and produces the best results.[16]

Like the men of his time, or perhaps like all men everywhere, Harper felt that what he wished to accomplish was foreordained anyway. His interpretation of the way of Nature was in terms of an ever-increasing progress. Just as in his interpretation of Old Testament history, he leaned heavily on the theory that later writers and later generations approached a clearer and purer knowledge of God through successive generations, so, too, he believed in the inevitability of progress, through struggle, through "survival of the fittest," and through discovery of elements of order in chaos.

> The laws of institutional life are very similar to those of individual life, and in the development of institutions we may confidently believe in "the survival of the fittest." . . . The purpose of suffering, is, therefore, much the same in the case of an institution as in the case of an individual.[17]

The future was bright, since progress was patently visible:

> Each century seems to have added largely to the number of those who have freed themselves from the thralldom of ignorance and

superstition, and thereby have gained a point of view which makes thinking a possibility. . . . Today, as compared with past ages many more are thinking into fundamental problems; but still more will tomorrow be thinking into these problems; for humanity is just beginning to enjoy the sweetness of liberty; and liberty is something a taste of which creates an appetite which not even Heaven can repress so long as legitimate satisfaction is denied. . . . We see, for instance, that the truth is possessing the minds of the masses in a more definite and tangible way than heretofore. . . . Every generation, being the heir of preceding generations, comes into an accumulated inheritance which actually compels wide, and consequently deeper, consideration of all that relates to life.[18]

One has but to discover the laws of Nature, in this best of all possible worlds, and follow them. "Nature has marked out the great divisions of educational work, and the laws of nature may not be violated without entailing great waste." [19]

Thus, with Nature firmly on his side, convinced that progress was inevitable and that the future pointed unerringly in the direction of organization and system, Harper was disposed to view the organization of his university not as an isolated event, but as a momentous step. Chicago was, by her example, to bring order out of chaos in American education.

Harper visualized and planned for a university that would control (both directly and indirectly) a system of "affiliated" academies and junior colleges, much in the same way that the control of various railroad "systems" emanated from Chicago. Some of these institutions would retain their fiscal independence, others would be completely dominated by the University's administrative hierarchy; but in all cases the instruction offered would be of the same pattern as that offered at higher levels in the University itself and in its professional and graduate schools.

Thus, although there might and should be a removal of the first two years of college instruction from the central campus of the University, the University should still control all of its branches so that the whole might be pervaded by the "university spirit." Far from divorcing itself from responsibility for the academy and junior college, the University should attract to itself other types of schools—nurse's training, library science, technology, as well as the traditional professional schools of law and medicine. Persons not reached by the formal instruction given in any of these institutions would still be offered an opportunity to become partakers of the University community through contact with one of the subdivisions of University Extension, and thus share the blessings of the "university spirit." Each type of educational enterprise, or distributional outlet, was to have a place in the University since through its control of them the University would reorganize them systematically and imbue them with its ideals of independent research and scholarship. The function of quality control was assigned to the University Examiner's office.

In a very real sense Harper was attempting to build an educational "Trust."

The Tents of
Righteousness

It is a curious fact of history that William Rainey Harper, who borrowed so freely from Chautauqua, never acknowledged any debt, nor did he ever name any of the buildings, quadrangles, branches, or subdivisions of the University in honor of the institution to which he owed so much. Thus, the effect of the Chautauqua movement on American higher education has gone unrecognized and unrecorded.

The Chautauqua movement is best remembered, instead, for the faintly gaudy era of the tent circuits—a period roughly synonymous with that of the Model T Ford. At the peak of its popularity, one or another of the circuits pitched its big brown tent in each of more than eight thousand United States communities, stayed five to seven days, and presented a fantastic variety of offerings subsumed under the general rubric, "Culture."

Although they borrowed the talent and profited from the enthusiasm of the original Chautauqua, the circuits were in many respects more closely related to the post-Civil War lyceum than to Chautauqua itself. Keith Vawter, the originator of tent Chautauqua, was manager of the Chicago branch of the Redpath Lyceum Bureau in 1904 when he decided to try tents:

> Not wanting to endanger the respected Redpath Bureau's reputation should he fail, he did not use its name. . . . so for this adventure he converted himself into the "Standard Chautauqua Bureau of Chicago." [1]

Mr. Vawter's feelings for the "respected Redpath name" apparently did not extend to the at least equally respected name of Chautauqua. The respect due the Redpath name was merited primarily because Redpath was the best of the many bureaus offering lyceum programs, not because the programs themselves were particularly praiseworthy.

The post-Civil War lyceum platform was far different from the lyceum movement of the early part of the nineteenth century. In 1826, in Millbury, Massachusetts, Josiah Holbrook founded the first lyceum, and the idea of popular lectures on a variety of subjects quickly swept across the nation. The Lowell Institute in Boston, Cooper Institute (now Cooper Union) in New York, and the Peabody Institute in Baltimore are lasting memorials to the strength of the lyceum movement. County lyceums were established in the years immediately following 1826, and a National Lyceum, with a headquarters and an annual convention, was established in 1831.[2]

The overnight popularity of the lyceum, and its rapid spread to the west and south, testified to America's readiness for this kind of education. Nehemiah Cleaveland, an early protagonist of the lyceum movement, wrote in 1830:

> The formation of associations where none yet exist very naturally claims our first attention. By those who have not yet witnessed the

process this is generally supposed to be a difficult task. They can not believe that a people long sunk in apathy as to every object of education and self improvement can, at once and by means so simple, be roused to feel an active interest in them. But the testimony of a hundred cases shows that it can be done.[3]

Advocates of the lyceum advanced two arguments, among others, in support of its uniqueness as an educational movement. Thomas G. Grimke, of South Carolina, said: "The Lyceum system interferes with no other scheme of improvement and is, on the contrary, auxiliary to them all." [4] Henry Barnard added: "The Lyceum in its various departments should take up the education of the community where the schools leave it, and by every help and means of self culture carry it forward to the end of life." [5] Both these arguments were to be advanced forty years later by the supporters of Chautauqua. In the interim, however, the catastrophic struggle of the Civil War put an end, at least for a time, to the lyceum programs.

The informal machinery by which lyceum lecturers had been guaranteed audiences, fees, and travel arrangements broke down during the Civil War. Sponsoring organizations, such as the Young Men's Association of Chicago, were disrupted by the enlistment or conscription of the majority of their members, and in many cases these clubs were never reactivated. Lecturers undertook to make their own arrangements, and frequently disaster followed. James Redpath, a former newspaperman then residing in Boston, observed the great Charles Dickens and his English manager Dolby, wrestling ineffectually with the details of Dickens' lecture tour of 1867–68, and determined to do something about it. He had known many of the great and near-great because of his experiences as a newspaperman, and his Boston Lyceum Bureau (later the Redpath Lyceum Bureau) became the chief booking office for such great names as Mark Twain, Josh Billings, Wendell Phillips, William Lloyd Garrison, Julia Ward Howe, and many others.

The Redpath Bureau had many imitators, but no equal. James Redpath earned a reputation for integrity, quality, and above all, respectability—this last, a prime requisite in that period. One of his great attractions was Anna Elizabeth Dickinson, "the Joan of Arc of the [Civil] War," of whom Redpath said wonderingly:

> There is not a particle of forced modesty about her and she is not afraid to say shirt or legs, and everyone feels as though they were sitting in the presence of a very chaste and pureminded woman.[6]

Entertainment values rather than educational values became paramount in lyceums following Redpath's lead. Now numbers of people existed whose livelihood depended on bookings. Since the "talent" traveled long distances, guarantees had to be greater, and only the large communities could support a Redpath winter lyceum. The time was long past when Ralph Waldo Emerson could accept an engagement for five dollars and three quarts of oats for his horse. Instead of the content of a lecture, the prosperous city dwellers of the seventies and eighties were more interested in its effect. They wanted to laugh with the humorists or thrill to the pyrotechnics of a fundamentally empty display of oratory. Wendell Phillips, by all odds the most adept at rodomontade, stirred them with "Toussaint L'Overture":

> You think me a fanatic tonight, for you read history, not with your eyes, but with your prejudices. But fifty years hence, when

truth gets a hearing, the Muse of History will put Phocion for the Greeks, and Brutus for the Romans, Hampden for England and Fayette for France, choose Washington as the bright consummate flower of our earlier civilization and John Brown the ripe fruit of our noonday; then dipping her pen in the sunlight, will write in the clear blue above them all, the name of Toussaint L'Overture! [7]

The Muse of History's exercise in penmanship has not yet occurred, and Phillips' bombast seems as empty as it is inaccurate. It was popular, however, and it made money.

Making money was not the purpose of the many "little Chautauquas." They had been organized by people who had no financial axes to grind. Their common purpose was to provide in their areas a program, long or short, that would copy in content, if not in quality, the original at Chautauqua Lake. That program was primarily ameliorative, concentrating on self-improvement through Bible study, secular study, concern with current issues, social betterment, and political reform. Other activities, such as healthful recreation, the enjoyment of music, and just plain fun, were always secondary and were considered useful because they contributed to the individual's effectiveness as a student.

Time and change are synonymous, however, and the desire for bigness—a constant in American life—made many managers of "little Chautauquas" eager to attract more people by securing "big names" for their annual summer assemblies. Professors from nearby fresh-water colleges might have interesting things to say, but as attractions they could hardly rival the glamour of the famous personalities who were available through one or another of the various lyceum bureaus. Many "little Chautauquas" hired these big names and their appearances created a most gratifying sensation and consequent publicity.

Logic dictated the next step. The "talent" pointed out to the managers they met in the summer that independent booking was wasteful. On the winter lyceum circuit, schedules were planned to avoid backtracking. A tour of short jumps between appearances was arranged by the central office; consequently, lower fees could be charged. This made sense. Accordingly, loose associations of "independents" were formed in order that better "talent" at a lower price might be secured.

Unfortunately for these combinations, other factors conspired to make them fail. For one thing, the independents were widely scattered. Usually they were not near cities and therefore transportation was a problem. Connecting links between major rail lines were not yet achieved by interurban trolley lines, and livery stables were the only supplementary source to rail transportation. Finally, most independent assemblies had chosen the same dates in the summer, and, like county fairs, these were now traditional and could not be changed.

The problem still intrigued one brilliant entrepreneur, however. Keith Vawter, the Iowan who had become manager of the Redpath Chicago Bureau in 1902, was certain that intelligent planning could bring financial advantage to the independents and also give his bureau a systematic outlet for the summer months.

So with map, calendar, railroad timetables, and his list of available Redpath talent, Vawter planned a new kind of summer season. He built a sample program with proper [*sic*] balance of serious lecturers, humorists, magicians, popular music companies, play-readers and a few famous preachers, to operate on an eight day schedule. . . . the first bold spirit to plunge into the scheme was Elijah B. Jones of the independent Chautauqua in Marshalltown, Iowa. Jones signed for a series of programs to open July 1, 1904, and in the agreement guaranteed a $2,000 ticket sale. Of total gate receipts, Vawter was to receive the first $2,500 plus fifty percent of everything above it; in turn, he would pay all talent and be responsible for their train fares and expenses.[8]

Vawter signed up fewer independents than he had hoped, so to fill out his summer season he hired tents and gave the show in four other communities. Thus casually was born the brief but fantastic era of tent Chautauqua.

The first venture lost money, but in his attempt to bring his "talent" to communities other than those supporting independent Chautauquas, Vawter had hit upon a very practical expedient. He had persuaded prominent members of each community to band together and pledge themselves to a flat guarantee; thus, the responsibility for promoting season-ticket sales was theirs. Later refinements of what came to be known as the "basic Chautauqua contract" included the provision that all single-seat sales at the ticket office accrued to the circuit operator, and season tickets were not issued beyond the number equivalent to cover the guarantee. Since each of the guarantors was individually liable for any deficit in the guarantee, the sponsors could be depended upon for a vigorous last-minute effort, almost always successful, to push season-ticket sales. Local support where it most counted was thus assured.

In 1907 Vawter tried again and was successful, and so were many imitators. Soon twenty-two separate tent circuits were operating in as many different areas of the United States, and the brown Chautauqua tent became a familiar summertime sight.

The connotations of wickedness and abandon that rural America associated with the theatre were not applied to tent Chautauqua. The name itself was a warrant of respectability, and the reputations of the personalities who appeared behind the Chautauqua footlights were above reproach. Even the hitherto suspect theatre folk were acceptable in the Chautauqua setting. If the Reverend Dr. Frank Gunsaulus, founder of the Armour Institute of Technology, and the Reverend Russell Conwell, founder of Temple University, could appear on the same stage that supported the Ben Greet players, then the Ben Greet players were Culture, and therefore not sinful.

To a typical American village, Chautauqua personnel were a fascinating mixture of the engagingly wholesome and familiar on the one hand, and the glamorous and exotic on the other. The agent and crew boys, nonperformers, were college-boy types, clean-cut, handsome, and manly, and the "talent" brought with them a breath of the great world— musicians from the concert halls of Europe, editors and travelers who had hobnobbed with the great, and the justly famous themselves, such as the Great Commoner, William Jennings Bryan, whose diehard supporters ("only one greater ever walked this earth and He never trod American soil") truly idolized him.[9]

Chautauqua Week was an exciting time for the people of an American town. Each summer, the Chautauqua agent was the first to arrive, usually a week before the scheduled opening. Whenever possible, he was the same person who had secured the signatures of the local sponsors to the contract several months earlier, and his first move was to call these persons together and find out how the advance sale of season tickets had been going. The meeting was held in the office of the chairman, usually the principal or superintendent of the public schools, frequently a civic-minded banker or merchant. The agent was not surprised to find the advance sale slow. He radiated confidence and enthusiasm and the sponsoring committee began to lose their apprehension.

Soon visible evidence of the approaching event began to appear. A huge canvas banner, properly ventilated, was suspended over Main Street, bearing the succinct message, *Chautauqua, August 20–27, 1912.* Smaller banners flew from the back curtains of local automobiles, and the Hupmobile or Ford dealers organized a caravan of new models, similarly bedecked, to parade the principal streets with horns blowing. If the roads were dry, the caravan would also visit neighboring villages too small or too unenterprising to have scheduled a Chautauqua of their own. Clerks in local stores wore badges that proclaimed, I'M GOING! or, I BOUGHT MINE! All the churches in the area urged attendance from their pulpits, the Catholic incitation perhaps a shade less strong than the others. Even though John McCormack, Bishop John Ireland, and Rabbi Stephen Wise were featured talent on one or another of the circuits, a strong flavor of Protestantism clung nevertheless to the Chautauqua name.

By Wednesday the agent's ready handshake and flashing smile were familiar up and down Main Street. If ticket sales still lagged, he set up a booth near the post office, and staffed it with the prettiest high school girls he could find. Gigglingly, these insisted that every pedestrian wear one of the I BOUGHT

MINE badges and were disappointed when the season tickets were all sold out.

Sunday morning's train brought the crew boys and the big brown tent. Crew boys were vacationing college athletes, and the town's younger element managed to be on hand to watch them set up the tent in a meadow near Main Street.

The big event happened late Sunday afternoon. Local bandsmen, town dignitaries, the sponsoring committee, and nearly everyone who was not bedridden crowded around the railroad station to see the first day's talent arrive. The operatic soprano, appropriately beplumed, flashed a dazzling smile as she paused a moment on the train step. A troupe of Japanese acrobats (*aren't they tiny!*) bowed charmingly in turn as they mounted the steps of the Central House carryall. Those nine straight-backed youths must be the "White Hussars"— and the leonine head and squared shoulders those of the famous orator, Russell Conwell! No starveling theatrical troupe or minstrel show that ever played the local opera house could compete in glamour with such as these!

Oblivious to the sneers of the sophisticates, tent Chautauqua flourished in the United States for more than twenty years. It was praised for having done more toward keeping American public opinion informed, alert, and unbiased than any other movement, and in retrospect the judgment seems fair. Traveling Chautauqua brought to the attention of millions of Americans an impressive number of new ideas and concepts, many of which might never have received the popular support that guaranteed their acceptance. The graduated income tax, slum clearance, juvenile courts, pure food laws, the school lunch program, free textbooks, a balanced diet, physical fitness, the Camp Fire Girls, and the Boy Scout movement—all these and many more were concepts introduced by circuit Chautauqua to communities that had heard of them—if at all—only from the occasional schoolteacher or minister who had had the good fortune to spend a few weeks at Chautauqua Lake. Dedicated speakers, consumed with fervor for a single idea, found circuit Chautauqua platforms most useful in convincing large numbers of Americans that "something must be done." Thomas Mott Osborne urged prison reform, Maude Ballington Booth begged understanding and help for ex-convicts. Frank Dixon asked that municipalities consider the city manager form of government. Marcus A. Kavanaugh, a judge of Chicago's Superior Court, pointed out forcefully the need for court reform. Jacob Riis shocked audiences with "How the Other Half Lives," and Harvey Wiley, formerly chief chemist for the Department of Agriculture, was convincing in his arguments for more stringent legislation against harmful preservatives and coloring matter in food products.

These were the years when rural Americans (and they were then a majority) took themselves and their government seriously. One of the most popular Chautauqua speeches of the era was titled "Responsibilities of the American Citizen." Specific phases of this responsibility were discussed by Senator Albert W. Beveridge, by Lincoln Steffens, Senator George W. Norris, Senator Robert La Follette, Eugene V. Debs, and a host of others. Men with a program of action found that in many of the eight thousand communities that sponsored circuit Chautauqua, more than half the residents bought season tickets. This meant that ideas presented during Chautauqua Week were argued and discussed in these communities a hundred times in the ensuing year. People went to a Chautauqua to be stimulated. They saw their neighbors there. They watched the color creep up the neck of the local banker when Debs castigated the financial interests, and they planned to be present when the banker got his next shave from the barber, an unreconstructed Populist. If Debs had spoken at a political rally, the banker would not have gone, and there would have been no argument to anticipate. But everyone went to Chautauqua.

Tent Chautauqua began to die when the great issues disappeared. Aside from the serious political speakers and the dedicated reformers, the circuits had relatively little of lasting value to offer. Dramatic offerings, although frequently presented by skilled performers, were innocuous bits of sunshine or foreshortened versions of Shakespeare. Good music was presented occasionally, but it was carefully sandwiched between quantities of rousing band music and familiar airs sung by various kinds of costumed groups. Most managers considered Hawaiians and Swiss bell ringers safer than operatic singers. Humorists and inspirational speakers rapidly mined out that particular vein of entertainment. Some of the titles of these talks were stultifying in themselves; "The Peptomist: An Optimist in Action" and "Laughilosophy" are fair examples. Brooks Fletcher, in an inspirational talk titled "The Tragedies of the Unprepared," was accustomed to remark that Jesus was the first Chautauquan. "How to" talks were plentiful—even "How To Be Happy." The titles often lent themselves to burlesque as readily as do some of those associated with today's popular "digest" magazines; "The Man Worth While," "The Man of the Hour," and "The Man Who Cares" were predictably dull recitations of the imperfections of the human species, capped by an equally predictable peroration urging on the universal good. What is worse, they started no barbershop arguments.

An unconsciously ironical benediction by Bruce Bliven was pronounced on circuit Chautauqua in 1924, at the height of its popularity:

> The pabulum provided from Chautauqua and Lyceum platforms may not be much; but it is all there is, at least until radio becomes a serious educational force—if it ever does. . . . Nowhere else under the quiet stars at this moment will you find a more characteristic expression of the American Idea.[10]

6 Difficulties

The manager of the various Chautauqua circuits never lost an opportunity to identify the enterprise with the original Chautauqua Assembly. Nineteen twenty-four was therefore announced, with considerable fanfare, as the "Jubilee Year," in honor of the founding of the movement in 1874 by Vincent and Miller. In each community in which a circuit played that year, appropriate ceremonies were observed, and at the end of the 1924 season, attendance stood at an all-time high.

This evidence of vigor, however, was as deceptive as the bloom of health on a consumptive's cheek. The 1925 season was disappointing on all circuits, and 1926 was a disaster. By midsummer of that year Keith Vawter, of the Chicago Redpath Bureau—the man who had started it all—found he had a net return for that portion of the season of only $345. With a shrewdness typical of him, he sold his tents and contracts immediately. Those who did not follow his example went bankrupt, and the last Chautauqua circuit ground to a weary halt in Nashua, New Hampshire, in 1932.

The collapse of circuit Chautauqua has been attributed to the swift popularity of radio, to improved roads and mass-produced automobiles, and to the advent of talking pictures. There is no doubt that each of these had an adverse effect on attendance, but what was essentially an art form would not have disappeared so rapidly and so completely for purely economic reasons. Technical improvements create technical obsolescence: good roads and dependable cars inevitably doomed the interurban traction companies whose future seemed so assured in 1910. An art form, however, remains viable as long as it has something to say, and by the early 1920's circuit Chautauqua was really saying nothing.

Tent Chautauqua's demise was due to the inability of circuit managers to reconcile two fundamentally opposite goals: they wanted to bring culture to the hinterland, and they wanted to make money. They thought the answer lay in expansion, in more towns on the circuit, a longer season, bigger names. Their once proud boast that no serious issue was ever barred from a Chautauqua platform was forgotten, and they concentrated on hiring crowd-pleasing talent. They were influenced in their judgment by our common American propensity for equating bigness with excellence, and so they failed.

At first glance, any parallel between Harper's University of Chicago and the failure of circuit Chautauqua may seem farfetched, but the parallel does exist. Both the circuits and the University were created with Chautauqua as the pattern, and although Chicago continues to occupy an important place among the great universities of the world, Harper did fail to realize there his announced intention to "revolutionize university study in this country." His ambition for the University and his dream of combining a great number of specialized schools and colleges into a coherent and unified "system" drove him into an excess of expenditure which alienated Rockefeller and dried up, for a time, the steady stream of the financier's contributions. Discouragement and ill health made the last year of Harper's life a gloomy period, in addition to which effective control of the University passed from his hands. Even before Harper's death in 1906, Dean Harry P. Judson, the acting president, had begun a program of reorganization and retrenchment that was in fact an abandonment of Harper's goals. Harper accepted the inevitable with dignity and fortitude:

> He [Harper] told me first, with perfect composure, that he had received his death warrant; and then added that it was doubtless for the best; that he had probably done for the University all that lay in his power to do, and that another man, with different conceptions and different ideals, might now serve it better.[1]

The record of achievement that Harper left behind him at Chicago would have satisfied a man less well-endowed than he with courage and imagination. In his writings, however, we can discern the scope of his ambition for American higher education, and the problems and contradictions that prevented the realization of that ambition. In a different context and at a later date, some of these contradictions were responsible for the collapse of the Chautauqua circuits.

When Harper had transplanted to Chicago his own concept of the organization that had proved so successful at Chautauqua, he added the principle of research, which he considered fundamental to the "university spirit," the capstone of his idea of a university. He saw in free inquiry and independent investigation a cosmic principle that transcended mere method; he conceived of it as fundamental in the operation of the universe. In a startling passage which clearly illuminates his faith in research as something tremendously more important than a mere tool, he wrote:

Palestine was a great laboratory. For its erection and equipment centuries were taken and the whole world was laid under tribute. Babylon on the one side and Egypt on the other made each its most precious contributions. The laboratory was furnished with all the facilities for working out the greatest truths of the greatest science, the truths connected with God and man. Indeed, the laboratory was built in order to afford opportunity for experiment, and to give instruction in respect to a single problem, and in this problem the greatest truths were involved.

The director of the laboratory had been its architect. He was now to guide the work of investigation and instruction step by step. This architect, this director, this master workman, we may note was God. Strangely enough, the director thought it best not to show himself in person; but, for the time, to do his work through laboratory assistants, or agents. . . . It was expected that they would furnish discoveries of new truth and new formulations of old truth for the use of those who followed them. These pupils, to whom so great an opportunity was given, were the ancient Hebrews.

. . . there were, in fact, many laboratories in the world . . . and there was no laboratory in which earnest and scientific work was done that did not have some contribution to make. . . . But in these other laboratories the facilities were not so good, and, besides, the director was not so near at hand. . . .

The Old Testament is a laboratory notebook kept, under the supervision of the director, by the laboratory assistants whom he employed.[2]

The statement epitomizes not only Harper's idealized concept of the function of research, but neatly ties in with his faith in the inevitability of progress and his rejection of an all-or-nothing belief in divine grace in favor of bit-by-bit revelation.

As a practical administrator, Harper's experience proved to him that there was a gulf between what ought to be and what could immediately take place. In theory, the cosmic principle of research was one which should pervade all levels of the University. In practice, however, it became apparent to President Harper that the research method of teaching was inappropriate for lower division students. His research-minded faculty, however, like the Director of the "Palestinian laboratory," failed to recognize any distinction.

> After three or four years spent in the work of research, they seem to ignore the fact that there is any other method of work than that employed by the most advanced students. They therefore employ university methods with freshmen and sophomores, and the result is an utter waste of energy and time, both for the student and his instructor. When, now, we add to this the insane purpose manifested by some of them (especially those who have been in Germany) to Germanize everything with which they come into relation . . . We have a combination of evils to which may be traced a very considerable amount of waste.[8]

Harper suggested a remedy for this kind of situation in "the admission of no man to the position of instructor whose ability to teach has not been absolutely demonstrated; and in the furnishing of such instruction as will, to some extent at least, exhibit the organized structure and relationship of the various departments of university work." [4]

This was, of course, a pious hope and a worthy sentiment. As a practical possibility, it was unrealistic. The policies that Harper had established in the beginning had resulted in the organization of a university community whose values were such that unless a considerable amount of attention were given to the shibboleth of research, preferment was not to be expected. Department heads had been chosen for their preoccupation with research; accordingly, they chose subordi-

nates with the same predilections. Upper-division and graduate courses, particularly the seminars, carried prestige; accordingly, Junior College courses were assigned to the newly
fledged Ph.D.s, who immediately sought, not to improve their
technique of teaching, but to gain leisure for research and
publication so that they, too, might grow in dignity and be
assigned a seminar. To reverse this trend would have been
a superhuman task even for an administrator who was convinced that the research emphasis was in itself a mistake, and
there is no evidence that President Harper ever thought this.

Closely related to President Harper's acceptance of evolution in the Darwinian sense as fundamental to the natural
order of things was his belief that the modern business enterprise of his day, because most recent, represented the highest
and best type of human productive activity:

> The democracy of Greece, and the democracy of a century ago
> in our own land, were stages in the evolution which has been taking
> place from the beginning of man's history on earth. Wherever the
> industrial spirit has prevailed, as opposed to the predatory, this evolu-
> tion still continues, and will continue until it includes in its grasp
> the entire world.[5]

As this "industrial spirit" comes into its own, it will, according to Harper, exhibit two marked characteristics—con-
solidation and specialization. To Harper, these are not
merely techniques; they, too, are cosmic principles, since
they are techniques inseparable from the larger concept of
evolution by the survival of the fittest. For the institution,
as for the individual, techniques of specialization must be
discovered, differentiation must take place, and then, by
association of differentiated parts, progress to higher levels
of organization may be achieved.

The great combinations of business enterprise, therefore,

will represent steps in the evolutionary process, and will rise to the dignity of exhibiting a principle that should be followed in other types of institutions:

> It is a remark of frequent occurrence that one of the common features of our present civilization is the emphasis laid upon specialism in every line of work. It is also to be noted that, side by side with specialism, and because of specialism, another prominent feature exists, namely, that of combinations and trusts, for it is only the specialists who combine. It was not until the day of specialism that combinations could occur.[6]

Harper emphasizes that institutions in general, and institutions for higher education in particular, are not faced by an infinite number of possible courses of action from which they may choose on the basis of which seems best. They are faced by a dichotomy; they may choose to specialize and combine—since that is the underlying principle of survival— or they may choose to commit virtual suicide. Circumstances, however, will inevitably dictate the former course, since "institutions, like individuals, move along the line of least resistance."

> . . . The small college, the college of the denomination, is certain to continue in the future; but it will sooner or later yield to the pressure of competition on every side and in every line, to the demands of economy, made more rigorous by the diminishing rate of interest . . . and join itself in close association with other similar colleges. The purpose of this association will be, in part, protection, but also, in part, greater strength. If it be asked how these ends will be attained by such association, it may be answered, in general, in accordance with exactly the same principles which lead men engaged in the same business, whether it is insurance or railroading, whether it has to do with iron or sugar or wool, to join hands for the prevention of unnecessary expense, for the avoidance of injurious duplication, for the sake of gaining every possible economy.

But how, it may be asked, will these principles operate in the case of colleges? With such association, and as a result of the understanding reached thereby:

There will come a better distribution of work among the colleges, and all will not undertake to do every kind of work; . . . The evils of competition will be mitigated; . . .

Such a relationship will be, in fact, a federation, and through this federation each of the interested colleges will be enabled to strengthen its faculties, for there is no reason why a strong specialist in a particular subject might not serve two or three institutions; . . .

Moreover, one may predict the close association of the smaller colleges, not only with each other, but also, in every case, with a university. The great advantages which will be found to accrue both to the college and the university in such association will bring this about; for, after all, institutions, like individuals, move along the line of least resistance.[7]

It would not be strange if an industrialist or railroad magnate had taken this position, since their activities are based upon the premise that individually and collectively men will everywhere seek personal gain. A university president, however, occupies his position because he believes, or should believe, that men can be persuaded through education to choose, not "the line of least resistance" but the paths of justice and truth.

In many important respects, Harper's personality resembled much more closely that of an industrial leader than that of a university president. The first dean of Harper's law school wrote of him after his death:

At first sight he seemed to a stranger to be nothing but a man of energy, of push, rather unattractive, a man whose success was almost inexplicable. . . . He had the mind and manners of a captain of industry, but he had the heart and soul of a scholar and a sage.[8]

Perhaps because mind and manners are more capable of objective analysis than heart and soul, Harper's friends frequently marked his resemblance to a "captain of industry." Goodspeed recounts approvingly the following anecdote:

The late Mr. Marvin Hughitt, a few months before his death, related to the writer a conversation he once had with President Harper. Greatly impressed with his organizing capacity, Mr. Hughitt had said to him:

"The fact is, Dr. Harper, you ought to have my position, that is where you belong."

"Why, Mr. Hughitt," said the President, very much astonished, "What do you mean?"

"Just what I say," answered Mr. Hughitt, "You ought to be President of the Northwestern Railway in my place. You could run it better than I can." [9]

The idea expressed is not a fanciful one, for in point of fact there is considerable evidence to indicate that Harper possessed many characteristics that would have made him successful in conducting a commercial enterprise. Paradoxically, these same attitudes were responsible for contradictions in the organization and management of the University that hampered its optimum development.

The organization of the University on the lines of an industrial enterprise resulted in overcentralization, rigid departmentalization, and loss of faculty morale. The attempt to utilize plant and staff on a year-round basis resulted in excessive duplication of courses and a loss in homogeneity in the student body. The emphasis on research as units to be produced undermined the faculty's interest in teaching. At the root of all these contradictions lay Harper's belief, unverbalized because implicit, that *demand* and *need* were synonymous. He interpreted the educational scene about him as indicating that the United States was in need of a unified and harmonious scheme of education, organized vertically from the kindergarten through the university, laterally by voluntary associations of colleges with one another and with a parent university, and supplemented by university extension courses available to everyone, the whole to be permeated by the "university spirit"—that is, investigation and specialization. Having been given an opportunity to do so, he had worked out such a system, and he remained supremely confident almost to the end of his life that that system would be adopted. In 1902 he wrote:

> The field of higher education is, at the present time, in an extremely disorganized condition. But the forces are already in existence, through the operation of which, at no distant date, order will be secured, and a great system established, which may be designated "the American System." The important steps to be taken in working out such a system are co-ordination, specialization and association.[10]

Harper believed that the essentials of the "American System" had been established at Chicago. As soon as some of the minor conflicts were worked out, Chicago would demonstrate to the rest of the nation the validity of his scheme, and it would be widely copied.

Had Harper been in fact an industrial or commercial entrepreneur, and had he evolved in that sphere such a logical and detailed plan for the distribution of a commodity, he could confidently have expected success. Perhaps his mistake was that he, like so many of his contemporaries, regarded education as a commodity. Thorstein Veblen, with his usual penetrating insight, perceived this assumption that underlay an education dominated by business ideals and business methods:

The underlying business-like presumption accordingly appears to be that learning is a merchantable commodity, to be produced on a piece-rate plan, rated, bought and sold by standard units, measured, counted and reduced to staple equivalence by impersonal, mechanical tests.[11]

Essentially the same mistake was made by the managers of circuit Chautauqua. They thought that theirs was a merchantable commodity, too. They became so engrossed in the problems of management and deluded by the mirage of bigness that they lost sight of their basic cultural mission. Their programs became "standard units," and they devised a system by which they could be "measured, counted and reduced to staple equivalence."

When tent Chautauqua had become a big business, Vawter and the other entrepreneurs devised a system of "quality control" whereby local managers on the circuit reported "audience reaction" to a central office after every performance, indicating how each part of the program had been received. If there were indications that a performer was doing something that was not entirely "safe," a more or less strongly worded "suggestion" from the central office would be waiting for him at his next stop.[12] It is more than unlikely that any suggestion was ever offered to such platform greats as William Jennings Bryan or Booker T. Washington, but by 1924, as a well-trained observer noted, "excessive liberalism is an extremely unlikely contingency. Conservative as are Chautauqua audiences, its managers are more so." [13]

This system of reports worked at cross purposes with the ostensible goals of tent Chautauqua. Just as Harper's emphasis on research and scholarly production inhibited too many professors in their teaching function, surveillance by local managers made crowd-pleasers rather than agents of culture out of too many performers. For the men and women who seriously advocated a program of action, there was no place at all; they might offend somebody in the audience. The "inspirational" speakers took over, and the once vigorous Chautauqua movement was drowned in a flood of pap.

Basically, Harper and the circuit managers shared the same philosophy, verbalized in Harper's case, tacit in theirs. It was that "institutions, like individuals, move along the line of least resistance." Harper deduced from this principle that combination and specialization would come as naturally and beneficially to educational institutions as to business enterprises. The circuit entrepreneurs deduced that their prosperity depended upon "giving the people what they want."

Both were wrong. Higher education has followed an older and surer instinct and has in some measure avoided the impersonality, fragmentation, and loss of human values that have been the curse of modern industrial life. The policy-makers for circuit Chautauqua discovered too late, if at all, that attempts to please everyone end by pleasing no one; a discovery that the television networks of our own day have yet to make. The "line of least resistance," whether erroneously deduced from the evolutionary process or adapted as mere expediency, is hardly a sure guide to progress in human affairs.

7 A Postscript

The Chautauqua Institution today enjoys a secure and seemingly permanent place in American life. Each year many thousands return to the shady and peaceful "Grounds" for another season of opera, concerts, lectures, study courses, and recreation. For more than eighty-six years this annual influx has occurred, and fourth-generation Chautauquans are as loyal to the venerable institution as were any of their forebears. The Chautauqua movement, however, has passed into history.

Theodore Roosevelt is reported to have called the Chautauqua movement "the most American thing in America." The Roosevelt ebullience would naturally choose the superlative; in point of fact, the Chautauqua movement was only a part, albeit an important one, of the most American thing in America—our continuing revolution.

In its time, the Chautauqua movement was a useful instrument for shaping changes in the fabric of our society. These changes helped transform a nation that seemed headed for a reign of plutocracy into a nation that could accommodate sweeping changes and yet retain its democratic institutions.

The Chautauqua movement was born in a troubled period not unlike our own. The American of the 1870's faced, as we do, a bewildering number of complex problems. There was the arrogance of the railroads and the trusts, a prolonged and severe economic depression, political corruption in city, state, and federal government, a "stolen" Presidential election (Hayes-Tilden), and a wave of bitter strikes which shocked the nation and created widespread fear for the safety and permanence of American democratic institutions. "The politicians gazed with stupefaction at the convulsive movement of the masses," according to a modern historian, writing of those times. The *New York Sun,* reporting the violence that accompanied the Baltimore and Ohio Railroad strike of 1877, said, "Hell is open and the lid is off." E. L. Godkin, editor of the *Nation,* concluded that a large standing army would have to be raised and maintained to put down the internal disorders which, he believed, would undoubtedly increase in violence and frequency.[1]

Godkin's remedy was European; Americans prefer to deal with problems by tentative, undogmatic improvisation. As Turner has said of the American pioneer:

> He was forced to make old tools serve new uses; to shape former habits, institutions and ideas to changed conditions; and to favor new means when the old proved inapplicable.[2]

Instead of looking to federal bayonets, Americans looked to themselves for solutions to the host of problems that beset them in the seventies and eighties. The Chautauqua movement lay ready to hand, and they used it. They subscribed to Chautauqua courses, copied Chautauqua forums, hired Chautauqua speakers, emulated Chautauqua ideals. As a "John the Baptist," Chautauqua paved the way for extension courses, community colleges, adult education centers, and dozens of other educational ventures, each of which took over a function of the Chautauqua movement until none was left. The Chautauqua movement served America well, and when its time was over, it withdrew quietly to its place of origin, where it continues to leaven the lives of many. Its contribution to our continuing American revolution was timely and considerable.

The great material advance of the past forty years has its place, too, in the continuing American revolution, but the gain has not been made without cost. The individualism which spurred so many to learn Hebrew, or to enroll in a demanding course of study, or to swelter in a brown canvas tent for the sake of "culture" is no longer a vital force in our lives. We tend to think of ourselves in terms of our membership in a social class, a union, a profession, a minority, or simply an interest group; we passively accept the group values, and thereby surrender our identity. Paradoxically, the issues of our times are presented to us while we are alone, reading our newspapers, or, more rarely, watching television, with no community of feeling between ourselves and the millions of other readers or watchers. We are passive observers. The shared experience of Lyceum and Chautauqua which produced excited discussions is no longer a part of modern life.[8]

Changed times must bring new improvisations. Today we

83438

need to improvise something that will meet our needs as the Chautauqua movement met those of an earlier time. Some way must be found to end the progressive loss of individual identity and to bring the great issues to the people as effectively as Chautauqua ended the stultifying isolation of rural communities and sustained popular interest in the problems of its day.

This should be the next development in our continuing American revolution.

Notes

I. BIRTH OF A MOVEMENT

1. Lewis Miller, co-founder with Dr. Vincent of the Chautauqua Assembly, quietly worked behind the scenes to make the new venture an efficient and financially stable operation. His title was Business Manager. Dr. Vincent was first styled Superintendent of Instruction and later Chancellor. There was never any question of rank; both men worked together in harmony and each supplemented the talents of the other. Leon H. Vincent, *John Heyl Vincent* (New York: Macmillan, 1925).

2. *Ibid.*, p. 55. Vincent sailed for Europe in July, 1862, with the purpose of attending the General Sunday School Conference in London. His itinerary covered Ireland, Scotland, England, France, Switzerland, and Italy, and he also visited Cairo, Jerusalem, Beirut, Damascus, and Athens. His conviction that a knowledge of history and geography was essential for a right understanding of the Bible stemmed from this experience.

3. *Ibid.*, p. 24. William Miller (1782–1849) founded the sect of Second Adventists (Millerites) and preached that the Biblical prophecies foretold the end of the world in 1843. On a particular night in that year, his followers in hundreds of communities donned white robes and crowded roofs and hilltops to await the cataclysm. When it did not occur, Miller restudied the prophecies, found his error, and fixed upon a date in 1844.

After the Millerite fiasco, there came a gradual shift away from terror as a means of religious conversion. Horace Bushnell's *Christian Nurture*, first published in 1847, held the position that "the child is to grow up a Christian and never know himself as being otherwise." First condemned as a heretic, Bushnell was later "recognized as the chief inspiration of the new liberalizing movement in religion and theology." Horace Bushnell, *Christian Nurture* (New York: Charles Scribner, 1860), p. 10; William Warren Sweet, *The Story of Religion In America* (New York: Harper, 1939), p. 491.

4. Helena M. Stonehouse, *One Hundred Forty Years of Methodism in the Jamestown, New York Area* (privately printed, 1954), p. 44.

5. *Ibid.*, p. 45. Although the publicity was of undoubted benefit to Chautauqua, the major political parties learned that candidates and office-holders also benefited greatly by news releases associating them with the integrity and high purpose of the new enterprise. After Grant, nearly every President visited Chautauqua at least once, either as a candidate or incumbent, and hosts of Congressmen managed to be invited to speak there. In 1913 "forty members of both houses addressed the Assembly." *Review of Reviews*, 50 (July, 1914) 53–59.

6. Zona Gale, "Katytown in the Eighties," *Harper's*, August, 1928, p. 288.

7. DeTocqueville found the American pioneer of 1830 anything but culturally underprivileged. ". . . he is, in short, a highly civilized being who consents for a time to inhabit the backwoods. . . . It is difficult to imagine the incredible rapidity with which thought circulates in the midst of these deserts. I do not think that so much intellectual activity exists in the most enlightened districts of France." Alexis DeTocqueville, *Democracy In America* (New York: Knopf, 1945), I, 317.

By contrast, the homesteader's lot was hard and discouraging. Turner writes: "It was a hopeless effort to conquer a new province by the forces that had won the prairies. The American farmer had suffered his first defeat. . . . [The] western pioneers took alarm for their ideals of democracy as the outcome of the free struggle for the national resources became apparent." F. J. Turner, *The Frontier in American History* (New York: Henry Holt, 1921), pp. 145, 305. See also F. E. Haynes, *Third Party Movements Since the Civil War* (Des Moines: State Historical Society of Iowa, 1918); Louis B. Wright, *Culture on The Moving Frontier* (Bloomington: Indiana University Press, 1955).

II. WILLIAM R. HARPER: YOUNG MAN IN A HURRY

1. The class consisted of three pupils. Dr. R. J. Miller, one of the three, who later took correspondence work from Harper, said: "I found that the system which afterward gave him an international reputation was but the development of principles and methods which he adopted in teaching that small class in Muskingum College." Letter to T. W. Goodspeed, undated (copy in University of Chicago Archives).

2. E. B. Andrews, *Biblical World*, XXVII (March, 1906), 168. The ties between the older and the younger man were very firm. In 1894 when Andrews, as president of Brown University, was at odds with his board of trustees, Harper wished to share the presidency of Chicago with him. The faculty opposed this move. This curious episode ended when Andrews declined the offer. "A Committee of the Faculty to W. R. Harper" (memorandum in University of Chicago Archives).

3. Eri B. Hulbert, *Biblical World*, XXVII (March, 1906), 172–73.

4. Rebecca Richmond, *Chautauqua, An American Place* (New York: Duell, Sloane & Pearce, 1943), p. 98.

5. R. S. Holmes, "The Chautauqua University, What Are Its Claims?" *Chautauquan*, V (April, 1885), 408.

6. R. S. Holmes, *Chautauquan*, V (November, 1884), 118.

7. John H. Vincent, *Brief Statement of the Chautauqua System of Popular Education*, Chautauqua Document Number I (Buffalo: Chautauqua Press, 1891).

8. John H. Vincent, "Honesty in the C.L.S.C.," *Chautauquan*, V (May, 1885), 472.

9. William Rainey Harper, *The Trend In Higher Education* (Chicago: University of Chicago Press, 1905), pp. 375–76. "The laws of institutional life are similar to individual life, and in the development of institutions we may confidently believe in 'the survival of the fittest.' " This belief seems to have influenced many of Harper's policies as university president.

10. Hulbert, *op. cit.*, p. 174.

11. *Ibid.*, p. 175.

12. T. W. Goodspeed, *William Rainey Harper* (Chicago: The University of Chicago Press, 1928), p. 49. Harper was always attracted to the idea that educational ventures could be self-liquidating.

13. T. W. Goodspeed to J. D. Rockefeller, April 7, 1886 (University of Chicago Archives). Other letters in the Archives that have been used in the preparation of this chapter are: J. D. Rockefeller to T. W. Goodspeed, April 13, 1886; T. W. Goodspeed to J. D. Rockefeller, April 22, 1886; J. D. Rockefeller to T. W. Goodspeed, June 14, 1886; T. W. Goodspeed to W. R. Harper, September 17, 1886; and S. H. Lee to W. R. Harper, September 5, 1887.

14. "It had never occurred to me but that you and the other standbys were permanent there and that in contributing to the Theological Seminary, *I was placing money where it would remain doing good for ages*" [*italics added*]. This is an excellent example of Mr. Rockefeller's concept of his stewardship.

15. Francis Brown, *American Journal of Semitic Languages and Literature*, XXII (April, 1906), 177.

16. Bernard C. Steiner, "The History of Education in Connecticut,"

Bureau of Education, Circular of Information No. 2, 1893, *Contributions to American Educational History No. 14* (Washington, D.C., Government Printing Office, 1893), p. 220.

17. Timothy Dwight, *Memories of Yale Life and Men, 1845–1899* (New York: Dodd, Mead, 1903), p. 470.

18. S. H. Lee to W. R. Harper, September 5, 1887. When this letter was written, Lee was 54 years old. A Congregationalist minister, he had been graduated from Yale in 1853. He had been dismissed from pastorates in Brockton and Greenfield, Massachusetts, had taught economics at Oberlin, and was currently preaching in New Haven, *Who Was Who In America, 1897–1942* (Chicago: A. N. Marquis, 1942), I, 717.

19. *Chautauquan*, X (November, 1889), 212. Dr. Vincent had been made a bishop of the Methodist Episcopal Church in 1888.

20. Herbert B. Adams, "University Extension and Its Leaders," *Review of Reviews*, III (July, 1891), 593–609.

21. Annual Meeting, Board of Trustees, reported in *Chautauquan*, VIII (March, 1888), 392.

22. "Minutes, The Board of Trustees of the Chautauqua Assembly, Akron, Ohio, January, 1889," *Chautauquan*, IX (March, 1889), 382.

23. "Development of University Extension," University of the State of New York, *Regents Bulletin No. 21* (Albany: University of the State of New York, May, 1893), pp. 214–15.

24. *Chautauquan*, X (October, 1889), 86.

III. The Baptist Dream of a Super-University

1. T. W. Goodspeed to J. D. Rockefeller, December 28, 1886 (University of Chicago Archives). Other letters in the Archives that have been used in the preparation of this chapter are:

J. D. Rockefeller to T. W. Goodspeed, December 31, 1886,
T. W. Goodspeed to J. D. Rockefeller, January 7, 1887,
W. R. Harper to J. D. Rockefeller, January 11, 1887,
A. H. Strong to J. D. Rockefeller, February 22, 1887,
A. H. Strong to J. D. Rockefeller, September 25, 1887,
A. H. Strong to W. R. Harper, undated,
A. H. Strong to J. D. Rockefeller, November 26, 1887,
J. D. Rockefeller to W. R. Harper, November 30, 1887,
W. R. Harper to T. W. Goodspeed, October 13, 1888,
T. W. Goodspeed to W. R. Harper, October 15, 1888,
W. R. Harper to T. W. Goodspeed, November 5, 1888,
T. W. Goodspeed to J. D. Rockefeller, November 13, 1888,
W. R. Harper to F. T. Gates, July 31, 1890,
T. W. Goodspeed to W. R. Harper, September 7, 1890,

W. R. Harper to T. W. Goodspeed, September 6, 1890,
W. R. Harper to Henry Morehouse, September 11, 1890,
W. R. Harper to Henry Morehouse, September 22, 1890,
T. W. Goodspeed to W. R. Harper, October 15, 1890,
T. W. Goodspeed to W. R. Harper, November 3, 1890,
T. W. Goodspeed to W. R. Harper, January 6, 1891,
W. R. Harper to J. D. Rockefeller, January 8, 1891,
W. R. Harper to J. D. Rockefeller, January 26, 1891, and
Henry Morehouse to W. R. Harper, January 31, 1891.

2. Allan Nevins, *John D. Rockefeller* (New York: Charles Scribner's Sons, 1940), II, 173. Bessie Rockefeller, oldest daughter of the financier, married Charles A. Strong, President Strong's son, March 22, 1889.

3. Andrew D. White to Charles D. Adams, May 17, 1878. J. S. Brubacher and S. W. Rudy, *Higher Education in Transition* (New York: Harper, 1958), p. 160.

4. Nevins, *op. cit.*, II, 209.

5. F. T. Gates, "The Need for a Baptist University in Chicago" (typewritten copy, undated, University of Chicago Archives).

6. These men were: Dr. William R. Harper; Dr. Samuel W. Duncan; Dr. Henry L. Morehouse; Dr. Alvah Hovey; President of Newton Theological Seminary, Dr. Henry M. Taylor; President of Vassar College, Dr. H. G. Weston; President of Crozer Theological Seminary, Dr. E. Benjamin Andrews; Professor of History at Cornell, the Reverend J. F. Elder; and the Honorable A. L. Colby. T. W. Goodspeed, "Report to Trustees" in *The President's Report, 1892–1902* (Chicago: University of Chicago Press, 1903), p. 496.

7. A copy of the rules that Gates formulated for his fund-raisers, dated April 20, 1891, is in the University of Chicago Archives. Rule 6 is interesting: "If you find him big with gift, do not rush too eagerly to the birth. Let him feel that he is giving *it*, not that it is being taken from him by violence."

8. Morehouse replied (September 11, 1890): "I will incubate upon it and if anything worth while is hatched out, I will send you the chicken." The chicken arrived September 17 in the form of a telegram: "Put one hundred thousand into splendid seminary building to be called Rockefeller Hall."

9. Harper to Morehouse, September 22, 1890: "I have a plan for the organization of the University which will revolutionize college and university work in this country."

10. Harper to Rockefeller, January 8, 1891. In today's context Harper's hesitation seems capricious, so far have we become secularized. Our own standards of "availability" for private or public office are concerned with attitudes to Moscow rather than to Moses.

IV. Chautauqua Goes to Chicago

1. W. R. Harper to J. D. Rockefeller, September 22, 1890. Harper's letter of the same date to Henry Morehouse, quoted above, is less restrained.

2. It has been assumed that Harper wished to work toward a purely graduate institution. This and other evidence indicates the contrary. As soon as the opportunity arose, he added the Chicago Manual Training School and Frances Shimer Academy in the face of considerable opposition.

3. *Official Bulletin No. 1* (privately printed for the University, January, 1891), p. 8.

4. There is no indication in the *Bulletin* as to how this was to be accomplished. Instructors, of course, would regard as equally desirable any formula that would eliminate unfit administrators.

5. "The University Extension Division," *Official Bulletin No. 6* (Chicago: University of Chicago Press [June, 1892]), p. 2.

6. *Chautauquan*, V (March, 1885), 538–39. In 1888 Chautauqua University Extension was announced, and would have been added to this list. See also John Heyl Vincent, *The Chautauqua Movement* (Boston: Chautauqua Press, 1886), p. 51.

7. "It is proposed, in the discussion of the University Extension Work, to offer courses of lectures in and about the City of Chicago." (*Official Bulletin No. 1*, p. 8.) The idea of a corps of instructors continually traveling to distant points and offering university instruction to all who wished it had evidently not reached maturity in Harper's mind.

8. "For the first ten years the principal emphasis was on the lecture-study work . . ." Floyd W. Reeves and Associates, "University Extension Services," *University of Chicago Survey* (Chicago: University of Chicago Press, 1933), VIII, 4.

9. *Official Bulletin No. 1*, p. 2.

10. W. H. Page to W. R. Harper, quoted in T. W. Goodspeed, *William Rainey Harper*, p. 148. The anonymous critic of 1896 anticipated the evaluation of university presidents to be made by Americans in the succeeding half-century. For the period 1904 to 1954, presidents of railroads showed a net gain in salary of 11 per cent, and university presidents a net loss of 26 per cent. Beardsley Ruml and Sidney Tickton, "Teaching Salaries Then and Now," Fund for the Advancement of Education, *Bulletin No. 1* (1955), pp. 29–47. J. S. Brubacher and S. W. Rudy, *Higher Education in Transition*, p. 367.

11. Unpublished first report. Dr. Strong would have disagreed. His concept of a university differed greatly from Harper's. In his speech as valedictorian of Yale's Class of 1857, he took a position he was to hold consistently the rest of his life: "How many a man, absorbed in one de-

partment of a science, has forgotten in his ardor that all are bound together and inseparable linked . . ." A. H. Strong, *Valedictory Poem and Oration, Class of 1857, Yale College.* (Published by the class. New Haven: T. J. Stafford, Printer, 1857.)

12. Charles Eliot, "The Aims of the Higher Education," in *Educational Reform* (New York: Century, 1898), p. 223. J. S. Brubacher and S. W. Rudy, *op. cit.*, p. 135, suggest that this concept of the role of the professor stimulated the growth of extracurricular activities essentially unrelated to the purpose of higher education: ". . . in the era of German inspired faculty impersonalism, the fraternities and 'varsity athletes gained ascendancy," The point is well taken.

13. G. Stanley Hall, *Opening Exercises. Worcester, Clark University, October 2, 1889.* (Printed for the University.)

14. W. R. Harper, "Ideals of 'Educational Work,' " *Proceedings, 1899,* National Educational Association, pp. 988–89.

15. *Ibid.,* p. 998.

16. W. R. Harper, "The Situation of the Small College," *Trend,* pp. 388–89. Other examples are contained in this volume on pp. 87, 324.

17. Harper, *op. cit.,* pp. 375–76.

18. *Ibid.,* pp. 44–45.

19. *Ibid.,* p. 84.

V. The Tents of Righteousness

1. H. P. Harrison, *Culture Under Canvas* (New York: Hastings House, 1958), p. 21.

2. "The American Lyceum," U.S. Department of the Interior, *Bulletin No. 12* (Washington, D.C., Government Printing Office, 1932), p. 27.

3. Nehemiah Cleaveland, "Lyceums and Societies for the Diffusion of Useful Knowledge," *Proceedings, American Institute of Instruction,* I (1830), 159.

4. Thomas H. Grimke, "Lyceums," *American Annals of Education,* V (1835), 197.

5. Henry Barnard, "Moral and Educational Wants of Cities," *Connecticut Common School Journal,* IV (1842), p. 25.

6. C. F. Horner, *The Life of James Redpath* (New York: Barse and Hopkins, 1926), p. 145. Mr. Redpath's curious grammar was certainly not intended to imply a condition contrary to fact.

7. Thomas Beer, *Hanna, Crane and the Mauve Decade* (New York: Knopf, 1941), p. 82. When Phillips wished to remind his audience that Daniel Webster was dead, he said: "The unhappy statesman, defeated, heart-broken, sleeps by the solemn waves of the Atlantic." The appeal of

this periphrasis eludes us today. Social historians of the future will perhaps be as baffled by our concern with the moods of TV's Jack Paar.

8. Harrison, *op. cit.*, p. 51.

9. Clyde Brion Davis, *The Age of Indiscretion* (Philadelphia: Lippincott, 1950), p. 38.

10. Bruce Bliven, "Mother, Home and Heaven," *New Republic*, 37 (January 9, 1924), 172.

VI. Difficulties

1. W. G. Hale, "An Address at the 59th Convocation of the University, June 12, 1906," *The University of Chicago Record*, XI (July, 1906).

2. W. R. Harper, "The Old and New Testament Student," *Biblical World*, XVIII (March, 1897), 161.

3. W. R. Harper, "Waste in Education" (read before the Regents of the University of the State of New York, June 27, 1899), *Trend*, p. 98.

4. *Ibid.*, p. 115.

5. W. R. Harper, "The University and Democracy," *Trend*, p. 9.

6. W. R. Harper, "Ideals of Educational Work," *Proceedings*, National Educational Association, XXXIV (1895), 996.

7. W. R. Harper, "The Trend of University Education," *North American Review*, CLXXIV (April, 1902), 456–65.

8. Joseph Henry Beale, Jr., "Memorial Address at Harvard University, January 13, 1906," *University of Chicago Record*, X (March, 1906), 19

9. T. W. Goodspeed, *William Rainey Harper*, p. 147.

10. Harper, "The Trend of University Education," p. 465.

11. Thorstein Veblen, *The Higher Learning in America* (New York: Huebsch, 1918), p. 221.

12. Bliven, *loc. cit.*

13. *Ibid.*

VII. A Postscript

1. The quotation is from Matthew Josephson, *The Politicos* (New York: Harcourt, Brace, 1938), p. 252. The issue of the *New York Sun* is that of July 23, 1877. Godkin's editorial appeared in the *Nation*, August 1, 1877.

2. Turner, *op. cit.*, p. 271.

3. The Fund for the Republic is at the present time supporting financially a number of centers for study-discussion. Groups organized by these centers are offered a number of study-discussion opportunities. Roundtable groups are guided by trained leaders and use motion pictures, recordings, and books as stimulation. The concept is reminiscent of the Chautauqua movement, and could become as valuable.

POSTWAR COLLEGE LIBRARY

WESTMAR COLLEGE LIBRARY